The Gospel According to Luke
Part Two

Luke 12:1–24:53

Michael F. Patella

with Little Rock Scripture Study staff

Little Rock
Scripture Study

A ministry of the Diocese of Little Rock
in partnership with Liturgical Press

Nihil obstat for the commentary text by Michael F. Patella: Robert C. Harren, *Censor deputatus.*
Imprimatur for the commentary text by Michael F. Patella: ✠ John F. Kinney, Bishop of St. Cloud, Minnesota, August 30, 2005.

Cover design by Ann Blattner. Interior art by Ned Bustard.

 This symbol indicates material that was created by Little Rock Scripture Study to supplement the biblical text and commentary. Some of these inserts first appeared in the *Little Rock Catholic Study Bible*; others were created specifically for this book by Clifford M. Yeary.

1   2   3   4   5   6   7   8   9

Library of Congress Control Number: 2018946224

ISBN 978-0-8146-6369-1   ISBN 978-0-8146-6394-3 (e-book)

DIOCESE OF LITTLE ROCK

2500 North Tyler Street • P.O. Box 7565 • Little Rock, Arkansas 72217 • (501) 664-0340 Fax (501) 664-6304

Dear Friends,

The Bible is a gift of God to the church, the people gathered around the world throughout the ages in the name of Christ. God uses this sacred writing to continue to speak to us in all times and places.

I encourage you to make it your own by dedicated prayer and study with others and on your own. Little Rock Scripture Study is a ministry of the Catholic Diocese of Little Rock. It provides the tools you need to faithfully understand what you are reading, to appreciate its meaning for you and for our world, and to guide you in a way that will deepen your own ability to respond to God's call.

It is my hope that the Word of God will empower you as Christians to live a life worthy of your call as a child of God.

Sincerely in Christ,

✞ Anthony B. Taylor
Bishop of Little Rock

TABLE OF CONTENTS

Wrap-up lectures are available for each lesson at no charge. The link to these free lectures is LittleRockScripture.org/Lectures/LukePartTwo.

Welcome

The Bible is at the heart of what it means to be a Christian. It is the Spirit-inspired word of God for us. It reveals to us the God who created, redeemed, and guides us still. It speaks to us personally and as a church. It forms the basis of our public liturgical life and our private prayer lives. It urges us to live worthily and justly, to love tenderly and wholeheartedly, and to be a part of building God's kingdom here on earth.

Though it was written a long time ago, in the context of a very different culture, the Bible is no relic of the past. Catholic biblical scholarship is among the best in the world, and in our time and place, we have unprecedented access to it. By making use of solid scholarship, we can discover much about the ancient culture and religious practices that shaped those who wrote the various books of the Bible. With these insights, and by praying with the words of Scripture, we allow the words and images to shape us as disciples. By sharing our journey of faithful listening to God's word with others, we have the opportunity to be stretched in our understanding and to form communities of love and learning. Ultimately, studying and praying with God's word deepens our relationship with Christ.

The Gospel According to Luke, Part Two
Luke 12:1–24:53

The resource you hold in your hands is divided into five lessons. Each lesson involves personal prayer and study using this book *and* the experience of group prayer, discussion, and wrap-up lecture.

If you are using this resource in the context of a small group, we suggest that you meet five times, discussing one lesson per meeting. Allow about 90 minutes for the small group gathering. Small groups function best with eight to twelve people to ensure good group dynamics and allow all to participate as they wish.

WHAT MATERIALS WILL YOU USE?

The materials in this book include:

- The text of the Gospel of Luke, chapters 12:1–24:53, using the New American Bible, Revised Edition as the translation.

- Commentary by Michael F. Patella (which has also been published separately as part of the New Collegeville Bible Commentary series).

- Occasional inserts 🔥 highlighting elements of the chapters of Luke being studied. Some of these appear also in the *Little Rock Catholic Study Bible* while others are supplied by staff writers.

- Questions for study, reflection, and discussion at the end of each lesson.

- Opening and closing prayers for each lesson, as well as other prayer forms available in the closing pages of the book.

In addition, there are wrap-up lectures available for each lesson. Your group may choose to purchase a DVD containing these lectures or make use of the audio or video lectures online at no charge. The link to these free lectures is: LittleRockScripture.org/Lectures/LukePartTwo. Of course, if your group has access to qualified speakers, you may choose to have live presentations.

Each person will need a current translation of the Bible. We recommend the *Little Rock Catholic Study Bible*, which makes use of the New American Bible, Revised Edition. Other translations, such as the New Jerusalem Bible or the New Revised Standard Version: Catholic Edition, would also work well.

HOW WILL YOU USE THESE MATERIALS?

Prepare in advance

Using Lesson One as an example:

- Begin with a simple prayer like the one found on page 11.

- Read the assigned material in the printed book for Lesson One (pages 12–21) so that you are prepared for the weekly small group session. You may do this assignment by reading a portion over a period of several days (effective and manageable) or by preparing all at once (more challenging).

- Answer the questions, Exploring Lesson One, found at the end of the assigned reading, pages 22–23.

- Use the closing prayer on page 24 when you complete your study. This prayer may be used again when you meet with the group.

Meet with your small group

- After introductions and greetings, allow time for prayer (about 5 minutes) as you begin the group session. You may use the prayer found on page 11 (also used by individuals in their preparation) or use a prayer of your choosing.

- Spend about 45–50 minutes discussing the responses to the questions that were prepared in advance. You may also develop your discussion further by responding to questions and interests that arise during the discussion and faith-sharing itself.

- Close the discussion and faith-sharing with prayer, about 5–10 minutes. You may use the closing prayer at the end of each lesson or one of your choosing at the end of the book. It's important to allow people to pray for personal and community needs and to give thanks for how God is moving in your lives.

- Listen to or view the wrap-up lecture associated with each lesson (15–20 minutes). You may watch the lecture online, use a DVD, or provide a live lecture by a qualified local speaker. This lecture provides a common focus for the group and reinforces insights from each lesson. You may view the lecture together at the end of the session or, if your group runs out of time, you may invite group members to watch the lecture on their own time after the discussion.

Above all, be aware that the Holy Spirit is moving within and among you.

The Gospel According to
Luke

Part Two

LESSON ONE

Introduction and Luke 12–13

Begin your personal study and group discussion with a simple and sincere prayer such as:

Prayer

God of all goodness, open my heart to hear you speak through the Gospel of Luke. Help me to journey faithfully toward Jerusalem with Jesus.

Read the introduction to Luke on page 12 and the Bible text of Luke 12–13 found in the outside columns of pages 13–21, highlighting what stands out to you.

Read the accompanying commentary to add to your understanding.

Respond to the questions on pages 22–23, Exploring Lesson One.

The closing prayer on page 24 is for your personal use and may be used at the end of group discussion.

INTRODUCTION

Introduction to the Gospel of Luke, Part Two (Luke 12:1–24:53)

Welcome to the second half of Little Rock Scripture Study's *The Gospel According to Luke*, which will explore in depth Luke 12:1 through 24:53, using the associated sections of Michael F. Patella's New Collegeville Bible Commentary, *The Gospel According to Luke*. The first half of this study covered Luke 1:1 through 11:54, and included the appropriate sections of the same commentary by Patella.

Luke is the longest of the four Gospels in the New Testament and it contains a number of Jesus' beloved parables that are found in no other gospel. Two of Jesus' best known parables are found in the second half of Luke: the parable of the son who squandered his inheritance only to be received back with great joy by his father, and the parable concerning poor Lazarus and the rich man who perpetually ignored him.

Whether or not you participated in the study of the first half of Luke, it is appropriate here to identify some of the pertinent themes of Luke that appeared in the first half of the study and that continue to be of importance as they re-present themselves in the second half. In his introduction to Luke, Michael Patella stresses four primary themes, or motifs, found throughout Luke.

First, Christ and his many miracles are depicted as a victorious force against the power of evil, personified in Satan.

Second, the coming of Christ into the world inaugurates God's plan to impose a great reversal in world affairs. The hungry will feast and the rich will grow hungry. The humble of the earth will be exalted while the mighty and the proud will be brought low.

Third, the motif of schism, the separation of people into opposing camps, is shown to be the inevitable result of Christ's teaching and activity. He offers God's embrace to all but a decision must be made to accept or reject his message, sharply dividing people in their response to him.

Finally, Patella says Luke's Gospel is riddled with joy. Those who accept Jesus' message and experience God's embrace are filled with great joy. For Luke, joy is the enduring mark of Christians.

12:1-12 In face of persecution

We last read of the crowds in 11:29. Mention of them here returns our focus to Jesus' preaching. The reference to the "leaven . . . of the Pharisees" (v. 1) thematically connects this scene with the meal at the Pharisee's house (11:27-54).

In verse 4 Jesus calls his disciples, and possibly by extension the rest of the people, "friends." This is the only occurrence in all three Synoptic Gospels in which we see this form of address applied to Jesus' followers, and it is another example of a tradition Luke seems to share with John (see John 15:14-15).

In a time of persecution, people generally go into hiding and maintain a secret existence. Jesus' admonition describes a situation in which no hiding will be possible, even if it were desirable. True fear should be reserved for the One who can cast a believer into Gehenna after the body is dead (v. 5). This phrase serves as a circumlocution emphasizing that we need fear only God.

"Gehenna" is a Greek transliteration of the Hebrew *Hinnom*, the name of the valley on the western side of Jerusalem. Often cursed by the Jewish prophets for the child sacrifice that the Jerusalemites practiced there, it is also called Topheth (see 2 Kgs 23:10; Jer 7:31-32; 19:6, 11-14). In time, the Valley of Hinnom functioned as the city garbage dump, thereby making it ritually unclean. In both Jewish and Christian canonical and deuterocanonical texts, Gehenna is the metaphor for hell. As Jesus makes plain in other parts of his ministry, we have a hand in determining our salvation by opting to participate in God's grace. He emphasizes that our salvation lies beyond the reach of any persecutor.

CHAPTER 12

The Leaven of the Pharisees

¹Meanwhile, so many people were crowding together that they were trampling one another underfoot. He began to speak, first to his disciples, "Beware of the leaven—that is, the hypocrisy—of the Pharisees.

Courage under Persecution

²"There is nothing concealed that will not be revealed, nor secret that will not be known. ³Therefore whatever you have said in the darkness will be heard in the light, and what you have whispered behind closed doors will be proclaimed on the housetops. ⁴I tell you, my friends, do not be afraid of those who kill the body but after that can do no more. ⁵I shall show you whom to fear. Be afraid of the one who after killing has the power to cast into Gehenna; yes, I tell you, be afraid of that one. ⁶Are not five sparrows sold for two small coins? Yet not one of them has escaped the notice of God. ⁷Even the hairs of your head have all been counted. Do not be afraid. You are worth more than many sparrows. ⁸I tell you, everyone who acknowledges me before others the Son of Man will acknowledge before the angels of God. ⁹But whoever denies me before others will be denied before the angels of God.

Sayings about the Holy Spirit

¹⁰"Everyone who speaks a word against the Son of Man will be forgiven, but the one who blasphemes against the holy Spirit will not be forgiven. ¹¹When they take you before synagogues

continue

Blasphemy against the Holy Spirit has been the subject of many and varied interpretations in history. In the context of Luke and Acts, it constitutes resistance to the Spirit-empowered spread of the Gospel. To stand in the way of God's plan brings doom.

Not even denying Christ in the face of danger and threat will bring eternal condemnation; only a sin against the holy Spirit has that power. The sin against the holy Spirit is the refusal of God's mercy and forgiveness when it is offered. Here, too, by having the choice to accept or reject the love of Christ, we have a role in determining our salvation.

and before rulers and authorities, do not worry about how or what your defense will be or about what you are to say. ¹²For the holy Spirit will teach you at that moment what you should say."

Saying against Greed

¹³Someone in the crowd said to him, "Teacher, tell my brother to share the inheritance with me." ¹⁴He replied to him, "Friend, who appointed me as your judge and arbitrator?" ¹⁵Then he said to the crowd, "Take care to guard against all greed, for though one may be rich, one's life does not consist of possessions."

Parable of the Rich Fool

¹⁶Then he told them a parable. "There was a rich man whose land produced a bountiful harvest. ¹⁷He asked himself, 'What shall I do, for I do not have space to store my harvest?' ¹⁸And he said, 'This is what I shall do: I shall tear down my barns and build larger ones. There I shall store all my grain and other goods ¹⁹and I shall say to myself, "Now as for you, you have so many good things stored up for many years, rest, eat, drink, be merry!"' ²⁰But God said to him, 'You fool, this night your life will be demanded of you; and the things you have prepared, to whom will they belong?' ²¹Thus will it be for the one who stores up treasure for himself but is not rich in what matters to God."

continue

presents Jesus' true role and ministry while offering an ethical and eschatological lesson.

The person who calls out from the crowd misunderstands Jesus' mission. The person errs by viewing Jesus as an arbiter whose judgment rests on interpreting the intricacies of a legal code. Jesus refuses to be cast in such a position, and he turns the table on the questioner as well as the brother. The issue, Jesus implies, is not who is right or wrong about the inheritance; it is about greed and avarice. If both exhibited less covetousness, one would be inclined to share with the other, and the other would not suspect that he was being cheated. Jesus' ministry is to the lost, and both brothers are sinners. His action allows the two to receive his message. No one loses, and both have the opportunity to enter the kingdom. The parable of the rich fool, which follows (vv. 16-21), illustrates the lesson.

At no point in his discourse does the rich fool credit God for the harvest. Furthermore, he never acknowledges that the bounty should have some purpose other than satisfying his own desires. Because he is so selfish and self-centered, he dies without benefit of both his wealth and God's love. With this parable, Jesus warns the two brothers to guard against ending up like the rich fool—a total loser. An example of how bad it will be for someone like this individual is found in the parable of the rich man and Lazarus (16:19-31).

God will not abandon those facing the sword. The holy Spirit will not only be present in fortifying the witnesses to Jesus but will also direct them in their actions and speak on their behalf, as Luke demonstrates in the Acts of the Apostles.

12:13-21 Greed and riches

This section consists of a dialogue followed by a parable. The first half, prompted by someone in the crowd calling out to Jesus, succinctly

12:22-34 Trust and faith in God

Matthew places this discourse within the Sermon on the Mount (see Matt 6:25-34), while Luke situates it on the journey to Jerusalem. Nonetheless, the lesson is the same: God's love is so abundant that he looks after every human need. In Luke, this passage provides the proper frame of mind and heart that stands in contrast to the focus of the rich fool seen above (vv. 16-21).

The Greek *korax*, translated here as "ravens" (v. 24), can also mean "crow"; in any case, it refers to a scavenger. Not only was such a creature forbidden as food to Jews, but it was considered a disgusting bird also among Gentile Greeks. Its repulsive character, therefore, makes the comparison all the more striking. Using the rhetorical form of the comparison of the greater, the listener or reader understands that if God tends to the needs of a repugnant carrion-eater, how much more will he care for his beloved people (see also Ps 147:9 and Job 38:41).

This same type of comparison is employed further on in the passage with the flowers, called *krinon* in Greek. Most probably it is the crocus, referred to in other parts of the Bible as the "flower of Sharon" (Song 2:1). Against the green Galilean hillsides in rainy times of the year, these blossoms give a dazzling appearance. Yet the spectacular color of the grass and flowers is short-lived. As soon as the weather turns warm, both the herbage and the blooms shrivel up. In a land with little wood, dried grass is often used for fuel. Once again we hear the comparison of the greater. If God shows so much attention to what ends up in the fire, how much more does he care for his people.

Luke introduces a social justice theme not paralleled in Matthew's version. The "inexhaustible treasure in heaven" (v. 33) comes from almsgiving. Luke underscores the lesson of the discourse with verse 34. If we make ourselves rich in the eyes of God, our hearts and motivation will lead to union with God both in this life and the life to come. Furthermore, by becoming rich in heaven, we relieve ourselves of earthly anxiety.

Dependence on God

²²He said to [his] disciples, "Therefore I tell you, do not worry about your life and what you will eat, or about your body and what you will wear. ²³For life is more than food and the body more than clothing. ²⁴Notice the ravens: they do not sow or reap; they have neither storehouse nor barn, yet God feeds them. How much more important are you than birds! ²⁵Can any of you by worrying add a moment to your lifespan? ²⁶If even the smallest things are beyond your control, why are you anxious about the rest? ²⁷Notice how the flowers grow. They do not toil or spin. But I tell you, not even Solomon in all his splendor was dressed like one of them. ²⁸If God so clothes the grass in the field that grows today and is thrown into the oven tomorrow, will he not much more provide for you, O you of little faith? ²⁹As for you, do not seek what you are to eat and what you are to drink, and do not worry anymore. ³⁰All the nations of the world seek for these things, and your Father knows that you need them. ³¹Instead, seek his kingdom, and these other things will be given you besides. ³²Do not be afraid any longer, little flock, for your Father is pleased to give you the kingdom. ³³Sell your belongings and give alms. Provide money bags for yourselves that do not wear out, an inexhaustible treasure in heaven that no thief can reach nor moth destroy. ³⁴For where your treasure is, there also will your heart be.

Vigilant and Faithful Servants

³⁵"Gird your loins and light your lamps ³⁶and be like servants who await their master's return from a wedding, ready to open immediately when

continue

12:35-48 The need for vigilance

The metaphors for vigilance all make the same point: the Lord's coming, or parousia, will happen when we least expect it. Each of the examples, however, gives a variety of views of what one can expect.

he comes and knocks. [37]Blessed are those servants whom the master finds vigilant on his arrival. Amen, I say to you, he will gird himself, have them recline at table, and proceed to wait on them. [38]And should he come in the second or third watch and find them prepared in this way, blessed are those servants. [39]Be sure of this: if the master of the house had known the hour when the thief was coming, he would not have let his house be broken into. [40]You also must be prepared, for at an hour you do not expect, the Son of Man will come."

[41]Then Peter said, "Lord, is this parable meant for us or for everyone?" [42]And the Lord replied, "Who, then, is the faithful and prudent steward whom the master will put in charge of his servants to distribute [the] food allowance at the proper time? [43]Blessed is that servant whom his master on arrival finds doing so. [44]Truly, I say to you, he will put him in charge of all his property. [45]But if that servant says to himself, 'My master is delayed in coming,' and begins to beat the menservants and the maidservants, to eat and drink and get drunk, [46]then that servant's master will come on an unexpected day and at an unknown hour and will punish him severely and assign him a place with the unfaithful. [47]That servant who knew his master's will but did not make preparations nor act in accord with his will shall be beaten severely; [48]and the servant who was ignorant of his master's will but acted in a way deserving of a severe beating shall be beaten only lightly. Much will be required of the person entrusted with much, and still more will be demanded of the person entrusted with more.

Jesus: A Cause of Division

[49]"I have come to set the earth on fire, and how I wish it were already blazing! [50]There is a baptism with which I must be baptized, and how great is my anguish until it is accomplished! [51]Do you think that I have come to establish peace on the earth? No, I tell you, but rather division. [52]From now on a household of five will be divided, three

continue

A master returning from a wedding would come with his bride (vv. 35-38). There would be feasting and celebration associated with the homecoming, which the servants should be ready to facilitate. In a role reversal, this master serves the servants. So too will it be at the eschatological banquet, when Jesus will be the host. The Lord's coming will arrive with the shock and surprise of a nighttime thief breaking into a house.

The notion of preparation introduces a paradox: this passage seems to contradict the parable of the rich fool (12:16-21). There readers are told not to worry about the morrow, food, or clothing, but here they are admonished not to take anything for granted, but to be ready for the unexpected. The paradox lies in the fact that adequate preparation is the result of letting go of worldly concerns and values. The prepared person will not be attached to the concerns of this life, even though she may be immersed in the midst of them.

The parable of the wise and just servant likewise has a strain of irony running through it (vv. 42-48). A good foreman will not take advantage of those under him, and if he does, the master will depose him upon his return. Such a punishment, however, is reserved only for the servant who knew his master's will and acted shamefully. The servant who does not know the master's will and commits the same actions will get off with a lighter punishment. The parable is a lesson in discipleship that parallels Luke 19:11-27. Followers of Christ will be held to a higher standard than nonbelievers.

12:49-59 Division, signs, conduct

Although this section appears to come from Q, verses 49-50 are found only in Luke's Gospel. The evangelist wishes to underscore that discipleship is not without its price, and the world will not gladly welcome the kingdom of God. Fire and water are both elements of destruction and cleansing, and as harsh as the imagery may seem, Luke uses them here to show the immediacy and totality of the impending *eschaton*. The more specific examples of how Christ's message will be received (vv. 51-53) depict a situation in the early church, most probably within the Jewish-Christian synagogues from which the Christians were eventually expelled.

In Israel and Palestine, rain can only come from the Mediterranean and only in the winter, hence the reference to the west wind (v. 54). Similarly, the Sahara, Sinai, and Arabian deserts lie in the south and are the source of the hot, desiccating breeze (v. 55). The signs of the times should be just as obvious.

This discourse works on several levels. The historical signs are the political precariousness of the Jewish state during the intertestamental epoch: Roman occupation, political dissension, and corrupt administration threatened the society to the point of anarchy. On the religious front, the signs of the times were Jesus' ministry (see Luke 4:16-21). These signs are the same no matter what the period in history. Issues of social justice coupled with the religious and spiritual emptiness are signs pointing to the eschatological reign. The Christian is called to respond to them.

The section ends with instruction to the early Christian community itself (vv. 57-59). As a people baptized in Christ's name, they should settle differences within the community and not resort to the pagan law courts. Christians have a new standard of behavior that encompasses personal behavior as well as ways of resolving injustices. These standards extend beyond restitution and include mercy, redemption, and forgiveness. Such an interpretation does not mean covering up shameful or wrongful behavior behind a cloak of secrecy; rather, it means making the community a living symbol of justice and reconciliation (see Matt 5:25-26).

13:1-9 Sin and repentance

The incident involving Pilate referred to here is one of the few places where he is mentioned outside the passion narratives, and it is very telling.

Many see Pontius Pilate as a weak, vacillating governor who feels overwhelmed by the vagaries of the mob, and, against his better

against two and two against three; [53]a father will be divided against his son and a son against his father, a mother against her daughter and a daughter against her mother, a mother-in-law against her daughter-in-law and a daughter-in-law against her mother-in-law."

Signs of the Times

[54]He also said to the crowds, "When you see [a] cloud rising in the west you say immediately that it is going to rain—and so it does; [55]and when you notice that the wind is blowing from the south you say that it is going to be hot—and so it is. [56]You hypocrites! You know how to interpret the appearance of the earth and the sky; why do you not know how to interpret the present time?

Settlement with an Opponent

[57]"Why do you not judge for yourselves what is right? [58]If you are to go with your opponent before a magistrate, make an effort to settle the matter on the way; otherwise your opponent will turn you over to the judge, and the judge hand you over to the constable, and the constable throw you into prison. [59]I say to you, you will not be released until you have paid the last penny."

CHAPTER 13

A Call to Repentance

[1]At that time some people who were present there told him about the Galileans whose blood Pilate had mingled with the blood of their sacrifices. [2]He said to them in reply, "Do you think that because these Galileans suffered in this way they were greater sinners than all other Galileans? [3]By no means! But I tell you, if you do not repent, you will all perish as they did! [4]Or those eighteen people who were killed when the tower at Siloam fell on them—do you think they were more guilty than everyone else who lived in Jerusalem? [5]By no means! But I tell you, if you do not repent, you will all perish as they did!"

continue

The Parable of the Barren Fig Tree

⁶And he told them this parable: "There once was a person who had a fig tree planted in his orchard, and when he came in search of fruit on it but found none, ⁷he said to the gardener, 'For three years now I have come in search of fruit on this fig tree but have found none. [So] cut it down. Why should it exhaust the soil?' ⁸He said to him in reply, 'Sir, leave it for this year also, and I shall cultivate the ground around it and fertilize it; ⁹it may bear fruit in the future. If not you can cut it down.'"

Cure of a Crippled Woman on the Sabbath

¹⁰He was teaching in a synagogue on the sabbath. ¹¹And a woman was there who for eighteen years had been crippled by a spirit; she was bent over, completely incapable of standing erect. ¹²When Jesus saw her, he called to her and said, "Woman, you are set free of your infirmity." ¹³He

continue

The lesson that Jesus draws from these events releases human suffering from the capricious judgment of wrathful gods, where many of then contemporary pagan cults had placed it, or even from known or unknown sinful behavior, as many in the Jewish religious establishment then taught. Instead, Jesus is saying that suffering comes to good and bad alike, and that all humankind stands in need of repentance and redemption. Someone's misfortune is not an indicator of moral culpability. John's Gospel (9:2) features a similar lesson in the healing of the person born blind (see also Ps 7:12-13).

With the parable of the fig tree (vv. 6-9), Luke employs a graceful thematic continuity from the stress on repentance to the value of the sinner. The fig tree is highly prized for the luscious texture and sweetness of its fruit (see Judg 9:10-11; 1 Kgs 5:5; 2 Kgs 18:31). Furthermore, the fruit can be dried and preserved for years on end.

The inedible variety of figs looks exactly like the edible kind. Moreover, edible figs can only be pollinated by the female fig wasp (*Blastophaga psenes*), which carries the pollen from the inedible fig and burrows into the buds of the edible one. Hence, for proper cultivation both types of fig trees are necessary. This delicate operation can confuse even the best gardeners, and patience is necessary to ensure a good harvest of the precious fruit. The lesson is that God will not give up on those who struggle with turning toward him. In addition, the great value placed on the fig tree characterizes the value of the sinner in God's eyes—not a reprobate or an outcast, but a prized possession, despite the possibility that the sinner may never "bear fruit."

13:10-17 The cure of the crippled woman on the sabbath

If Jesus was teaching in the synagogue, he must have originally met with respect from the synagogue leader. In fact, the leader reprimands not Jesus but the crowd of people who seemingly have come on the sabbath to be cured. The cause of the leader's discomfort,

judgment, he hands Jesus over to be crucified (see Matt 27:26; Mark 15:15; Luke 23:25; John 19:16). Luke's narrative counters such an assessment by relating this slaughter, for which there is no other record in the Bible or any other extant work. Josephus refers to an uprising of Jews when Pilate uses temple money to build a Jerusalem aqueduct (*Ant.* 18.3.2 and *J.W.* 2.9.4). Pilate ruthlessly suppresses the tumult by having disguised, weapon-bearing Roman soldiers mixed among the Jews. At a given signal, they begin to hack away at the civilian population.

It is quite plausible that both Josephus and Jesus are referring to the same calamity. Likewise, along the southeastern wall of ancient Jerusalem are visible ruins from a collapsed tower (v. 4) dating to the intertestamental period, that is, the two centuries between the composition of the last book of the Old Testament and the first book of the New Testament.

therefore, is not that Jesus cured but that this curing occurred on the Lord's Day. Healing was seen as work and therefore prohibited. Jesus uses this opportunity to make several points about his identity, his reign, and the world.

The Jewish sabbath, since it commemorates the seventh day on which God rested from all his labors, is literally the Lord's Day. Because of the holy character of the sabbath, the regulations against work were intended to give everyone access to this life in the Lord. Judging from Jesus' response, it appears that in this situation, the sabbath regulations had ceased to provide the spiritual renewal that originally had been associated with them. Jesus' challenge to the custom is successful only because of his authority. He thus gives the sabbath an eschatological dimension. Access to life in the Lord now becomes a foretaste of the heavenly realm, where sin and suffering are put to rout. This interpretation is evident in Jesus' reply (v. 16).

The reference to Satan in verse 16, combined with the setting of the cure on the sabbath, characterizes a central aspect of Lukan eschatology. Sickness and malady are viewed as a part of Satan's malevolent realm, which has made inroads into God's creation. Jesus' role is to redeem creation, to win it back for God. Jesus overpowers the evil forces and ushers in the eschatological reign. No longer dominated by Satan, the crippled woman now has her sabbath rest.

13:18-19 The parable of the mustard seed

All three Synoptics show this parable. The mustard seed was considered the smallest of all possible seeds. The tree itself, the *brassica nigra*, grows wild throughout Palestine and Israel, but farmers also cultivate it. With small, bright yellow flowers and slender, dark green leaves, it can grow to a large, many-branched shrub or tree. As such, it is a metaphor for the small early Christian community, which has an influence on the world going far beyond its size and number to the point that others (symbolized by birds) make their home in it.

laid his hands on her, and she at once stood up straight and glorified God. [14]But the leader of the synagogue, indignant that Jesus had cured on the sabbath, said to the crowd in reply, "There are six days when work should be done. Come on those days to be cured, not on the sabbath day." [15]The Lord said to him in reply, "Hypocrites! Does not each one of you on the sabbath untie his ox or his ass from the manger and lead it out for watering? [16]This daughter of Abraham, whom Satan has bound for eighteen years now, ought she not to have been set free on the sabbath day from this bondage?" [17]When he said this, all his adversaries were humiliated; and the whole crowd rejoiced at all the splendid deeds done by him.

The Parable of the Mustard Seed

[18]Then he said, "What is the kingdom of God like? To what can I compare it? [19]It is like a mustard seed that a person took and planted in the garden. When it was fully grown, it became a large bush and 'the birds of the sky dwelt in its branches.'"

The Parable of the Yeast

[20]Again he said, "To what shall I compare the kingdom of God? [21]It is like yeast that a woman took and mixed [in] with three measures of wheat flour until the whole batch of dough was leavened."

continue

13:20-21 The measure of yeast

This parable appears only in Matthew and Luke. The bread of the time would have been sourdough, as most bread was until the development of dry yeast. Once the dough was kneaded, pieces were pulled away, flattened, and laid over a hot metal dome called a *tamboun*. The result was a large, circular crêpe or pita.

Not much yeast was needed to cause a batch of dough to rise, so, like the parable of the mustard seed, the leaven stands as a measure for the Christian community. In this parable the woman who adds the yeast to the flour is the Christ figure.

What **kind of yeast** did the ancient Israelites use to leaven their bread? Usually, they made a type of sourdough bread, in which fermented dough from a previous batch of bread provided the leavening agent to make a new batch of bread rise. But during the feast of unleavened bread, all leavening agents were to be removed from the house (see Exod 12:15). In order to make new leavened bread following the feast of unleavened bread, more than one strategy could be employed. One would be to use some fruit juice in place of water alone to make dough, which would quickly ferment and create a new batch of sour dough. Another strategy would be to simply acquire leaven from a non-Jewish neighbor or merchant. Eventually, even unleavened dough left over from the feast of unleavened bread, perhaps stored in an earthen jar to preserve its moisture, would naturally ferment, providing a continuing source of leaven (wild yeast and lactobacilli).

13:22-30 The narrow door, salvation, and rejection

With this parable Jesus indirectly answers the question put to him. Restrictions to entering the kingdom do not lie with God but with the human response to the divine invitation. Because Luke recapitulates the point that Jesus is on his way to Jerusalem (v. 22), many consider this section as the beginning of the second half of the journey narrative leading to the city of his death and resurrection.

The conventional city gate during this period had one wide, high central arch flanked by two lower, narrower portals. The main arch permitted camels, carts, and goods to pass. Those who wished to enter and who had no baggage trains could avoid the traffic by walking through either one of the narrow gates.

Applying this daily occurrence to the parable, the lesson seems to be directed to those who drag along their religious or social status, their material possessions, or their own ambitions in seeking easy access to salvation. Jesus counters this attitude by extracting a lesson from a familiar scene. Just as today those who travel light reach their destination more easily than those with much luggage, so too will those who keep their eyes and actions on salvation find the swifter path through the smaller doors. Any attempt to interpret these verses as showing that Gentiles are saved at the expense of the Jews is based on a faulty reading. The setting of the story is Jesus' trip to Jerusalem accompanied by his Jewish disciples, but the Lukan community to whom this story is told is composed mostly of Gentiles. All are instructed, therefore, to enter by the narrow gate, a passage that is difficult but not impossible.

The introduction of mixed metaphors in verses 25-30 is a result of various strands of tradition redacted into one parable. The second lesson is similar to the first: one should not rely on status to enter the kingdom. To use a modern parallel, ticket holders who arrive for a concert at the last minute may still not get in if there is a long line at the gate; their reliance on their ticket stubs proves to be no guarantee of entry. If they had been earnest in their desire, they would have arrived early and waited in line to be sure of getting a seat.

13:31-33 The Pharisees warn about Herod

Do the Pharisees come to Jesus as friends and allies, or are they simply trying to frighten Jesus into submission? In either case, Jesus does not alter his intention to head to Jerusalem. Indeed, he uses the occasion to affirm it—he must go to Jerusalem (v. 33).

Lukan eschatology once again surfaces with the blending of three statements in verse 32. As in the parable of the crippled woman (13:10-17), curing the sick is seen as a successful assault on demonic forces. Furthermore, contained in this statement is a reference to Jesus' passion, death, and resurrection: "On the third day I accomplish my purpose" (v. 32). Jesus predicts his own death with his emphatic resolution to continue to Jerusalem, though, ironically, by traveling to Jerusalem he leaves Herod's jurisdiction.

13:34-35 The lament over Jerusalem

This passage, a rhetorical apostrophe, flows from the scene with the Pharisees immediately above and is a fine example of Luke's narrative finesse. Matthew's Gospel contains a parallel account, but in that Gospel Jesus utters these words after the triumphant entry into Jerusalem (see Matt 23:37-39).

In 13:33 Jesus says that a prophet should not die outside Jerusalem. His words over the city have him identifying with that destiny, and he does so by using a lament, a prophetic genre seen most clearly in Jeremiah and Lamentations. To be sure, prophets were also slain outside Jerusalem, but given the presence of the temple within the city and the city's history with the prophets, Jeremiah and Isaiah make Jerusalem the major symbol of a prophet's destiny (see 1 Kgs 9:7-8; 2 Kgs 21:16; Ps 118:2; Jer 22:5).

you are from.' [26] And you will say, 'We ate and drank in your company and you taught in our streets.' [27] Then he will say to you, 'I do not know where [you] are from. Depart from me, all you evildoers!' [28] And there will be wailing and grinding of teeth when you see Abraham, Isaac, and Jacob and all the prophets in the kingdom of God and you yourselves cast out. [29] And people will come from the east and the west and from the north and the south and will recline at table in the kingdom of God. [30] For behold, some are last who will be first, and some are first who will be last."

Herod's Desire to Kill Jesus

[31] At that time some Pharisees came to him and said, "Go away, leave this area because Herod wants to kill you." [32] He replied, "Go and tell that fox, 'Behold, I cast out demons and I perform healings today and tomorrow, and on the third day I accomplish my purpose. [33] Yet I must continue on my way today, tomorrow, and the following day, for it is impossible that a prophet should die outside of Jerusalem.'

The Lament over Jerusalem

[34] "Jerusalem, Jerusalem, you who kill the prophets and stone those sent to you, how many times I yearned to gather your children together as a hen gathers her brood under her wings, but you were unwilling! [35] Behold, your house will be abandoned. [But] I tell you, you will not see me until [the time comes when] you say, 'Blessed is he who comes in the name of the Lord.'"

In verse 34 the reader should note the feminine imagery inherent in Jesus' self-referential term "hen" (see also Deut 32:11). Contained also is the allusion to his entering the city in 19:28-40.

EXPLORING LESSON ONE

1. In what ways have you been personally challenged to acknowledge Jesus before others (12:2-9)?

_____

_____

_____

_____

2. Considering the ways you invest your time, energy, and money, what do see that you value most in life (12:13-34)? (See Matt 6:33; Gal 5:22.)

_____

_____

_____

_____

3. How has God asked you to serve others (12:35-48)? In what ways are you challenged to be vigilant in your service?

_____

_____

_____

_____

4. Where have you seen or experienced division or contention arising from faithfulness to Christ (12:49-53)?

_____

_____

_____

_____

5. How has your faith led you to respond or react to tragic events in the world (13:1-5)? Think of some concrete examples.

_____

_____

_____

_____

_____

6. a) What do you think the parable of the barren fig tree says about God's patience (13:6-9)?

_____

_____

_____

_____

   b) Where in your life is your own patience being developed?

_____

_____

_____

_____

7. Jesus compares the expansion of God's kingdom to both the growth of a mustard seed and the effect of yeast in bread dough (13:18-21). To what would you compare the development of faith in your own life?

_____

_____

_____

_____

8. The commentary states that entering salvation through the narrow gate is difficult but not impossible. What does it mean to you to strive to enter through the narrow gate (13:22-30)?

_____

_____

_____

_____

9. In both the parable of the yeast (13:20-21) and when Jesus weeps over Jerusalem (13:34-35) he uses feminine imagery to describe his ministry. In what ways have you experienced God's love as something maternal or feminine? (See Luke 15:8-10; 1 Thess 2:7; Sir 14:20–15:6; Isa 66:13.)

_____

_____

_____

_____

_____

CLOSING PRAYER

Prayer

"Woman you are set free of your infirmity."
(Luke 13:12)

You teach us, Jesus, that you desire wholeness and free-dom for each of us. Your word has the power to heal and liberate. We pray now for those in our families and neighborhoods who need to hear your healing voice, especially those we name . . .

LESSON TWO

Luke 14–16

Begin your personal study and group discussion with a simple and sincere prayer such as:

Prayer

God of all goodness, open my heart to hear you speak through the Gospel of Luke. Help me to journey faithfully toward Jerusalem with Jesus.

Read the Bible text of Luke 14–16 found in the outside columns of pages 26–35, highlighting what stands out to you.

Read the accompanying commentary to add to your understanding.

Respond to the questions on pages 37–38, Exploring Lesson Two.

The closing prayer on page 39 is for your personal use and may be used at the end of group discussion.

CHAPTER 14

Healing of the Man with Dropsy on the Sabbath

[1]On a sabbath he went to dine at the home of one of the leading Pharisees, and the people there were observing him carefully. [2]In front of him there was a man suffering from dropsy. [3]Jesus spoke to the scholars of the law and Pharisees in reply, asking, "Is it lawful to cure on the sabbath or not?" [4]But they kept silent; so he took the man and, after he had healed him, dismissed him. [5]Then he said to them, "Who among you, if your son or ox falls into a cistern, would not immediately pull him out on the sabbath day?" [6]But they were unable to answer his question.

Conduct of Invited Guests and Hosts

[7]He told a parable to those who had been invited, noticing how they were choosing the places of honor at the table. [8]"When you are invited by someone to a wedding banquet, do not recline at table in the place of honor. A more distinguished guest than you may have been invited by him, [9]and the host who invited both of you may approach you and say, 'Give your place to this man,' and then you would proceed with embarrassment to take the lowest place. [10]Rather, when you are invited, go and take the lowest place so that when the host comes to you he may say, 'My friend, move up to a higher position.' Then you will enjoy the esteem of your companions at the table. [11]For everyone who exalts himself will be humbled, but the one who humbles himself will be exalted."

continue

in both cases the miracle occurs on the sabbath. The woman is cured in front of the synagogue leaders, and the man here is restored to health in the presence of leading Pharisees. Furthermore, neither the woman nor the man asks Jesus to be healed; rather, in both instances Jesus, moved by pity, takes the initiative to cure the individual. He explains his action using the rhetorical device of the comparison of the greater: if the Law makes allowances for saving livestock on the sabbath, how much more should one help a fellow human being on the holy day.

Unlike the passage about the woman, however, there is nothing in this story to indicate that the leaders were angry or that they had duplicitous intentions in "observing him carefully" (v. 1). It seems that the Pharisees here are indeed curious about how Jesus would handle such a case, and, he engages them with his question (v. 3). Because they, too, know the Law and its provisions, they remain silent. Once again, the sabbath setting connects physical well-being with eternal salvation, thereby giving the Lord's Day an eschatological dimension (see also Luke 6:1-11; 11:37-54).

14:1-6 Healing a man with dropsy on the sabbath

Dropsy, or edema, is characterized by a buildup of fluids, often in the extremities. It is usually symptomatic of a variety of diseases.

There are several similarities between this story and the account of the crippled woman (13:10-17). They are solely Lukan material, and

14:7-14 Proper comportment of guests and hosts

With the man now cured of his dropsy, Luke continues to describe the action surrounding the dinner. Jesus observes the customs of courtesy and etiquette and ties these issues of daily protocol to a lesson about the kingdom. Luke calls this lesson a "parable" (v. 7), but its genre is closer to a wisdom saying. Only Luke contains this passage, although a parallel to verse 11 appears in Matthew 23:12, making this aphorism most probably a Q saying. It is also found in Luke 18:14.

The dining room would have been a *triclinium* (see 7:36-50). The host would recline on his left side at the top of the right extension of the table; the opening to the horseshoe-shaped construction would have been to his back. The place of honor would have been at the crossbar, making the position of the honored guest directly perpendicular to the host so that they could talk directly to each other. Succeeding places of honor continued along the crossbar and down the left side, with the lowest place situated at the end of the left extension; the guest would have to constantly readjust his position in order to converse with those in the lowest places. What Jesus notices, therefore, is a stream of guests jockeying for the spot perpendicular to the host while avoiding anything along the left extension, especially the last place.

In the Mediterranean world, an honor-shame based culture, the social gaffe of overstepping one's station, such as Jesus describes, would have been a mortifying experience. On the other hand, being asked to come higher would have been particularly enviable. The lesson goes beyond calculating a social standing among one's peers, however, and points to the proper disposition toward God and how we define our need for God's salvation in our lives. Social self-inflation is equated with spiritual self-righteousness. Those who assume that they are righteous enough to let themselves into the kingdom without any regard for the divine initiative will have to give way to those who know their unworthiness and depend on God's love and grace for everything.

Jesus then turns the lesson to the host. The Roman world ran on the patronage system, in which the rich and influential would curry favor among their constituencies in return for

> [12]Then he said to the host who invited him, "When you hold a lunch or a dinner, do not invite your friends or your brothers or your relatives or your wealthy neighbors, in case they may invite you back and you have repayment. [13]Rather, when you hold a banquet, invite the poor, the crippled, the lame, the blind; [14]blessed indeed will you be because of their inability to repay you. For you will be repaid at the resurrection of the righteous."
>
> ### The Parable of the Great Feast
>
> [15]One of his fellow guests on hearing this said to him, "Blessed is the one who will dine in the kingdom of God." [16]He replied to him, "A man gave a great dinner to which he invited many. [17]When the time for the dinner came, he dispatched his servant to say to those invited, 'Come,
>
> *continue*

support, respect, and fulfilled obligations. In such a society, a family holding a lavish banquet for notable dignitaries and lesser functionaries would be renowned for their generosity and would thereby garner a great deal of influence in their local area. Such would be their payback.

The true act of generosity in the eyes of God, however, lies in bestowing respect and dignity on those who would not only be unable to repay in kind but whose very social standing carries no prestige whatsoever. The reward one gains in the resurrection of the righteous (Greek: *dikaios*) ties this lesson to the one Jesus teaches to the guests (v. 14). In both instances, then, humility before God becomes the proper comportment for entering the kingdom.

14:15-24 The parable of the great banquet

This parable originates in Q and has a parallel in Matthew (22:1-14).

Banquets in the Gospel tradition always contain a strong eschatological element. Luke's creativity shines in this passage as he situates the banquet parable within the setting of a everything is now ready.' ¹⁸But one by one, they all began to excuse themselves. The first said to him, 'I have purchased a field and must go to examine it; I ask you, consider me excused.' ¹⁹And another said, 'I have purchased five yoke of oxen and am on my way to evaluate them; I ask you, consider me excused.' ²⁰And another said, 'I have just married a woman, and therefore I cannot come.' ²¹The servant went and reported this to his master. Then the master of the house in a rage commanded his servant, 'Go out quickly into the streets and alleys of the town and bring in here the poor and the crippled, the blind and the lame.' ²²The servant reported, 'Sir, your orders have been carried out and still there is room.' ²³The master then ordered the servant, 'Go out to the highways and hedgerows and make people come in that my home may be filled. ²⁴For, I tell you, none of those men who were invited will taste my dinner.' "

Sayings on Discipleship

²⁵Great crowds were traveling with him, and he turned and addressed them, ²⁶"If anyone comes to me without hating his father and mother, wife

continue

large dinner and gracefully folds the parable into the scene with the guest's remark in verse 15. The excuses that the original invitees give for not going to the dinner are legitimate. A wedding feast would last for several days, and one who has purchased land or cattle would have a strong desire to examine the sources of his livelihood. But these mitigating circumstances arise after they have presumably already accepted the invitation; it is the summons to enter the feast that they refuse. In a society in which a patronage system governs many areas of life, their refusals are a disrespectful insult to the host's generosity.

Moreover, the last excuses introduce an eschatological dimension. According to Deuteronomic law, those who have built a house, planted a vineyard, or married a woman did not have to go on a military expedition or engage in any public duty for a period of one year (Deut 20:5-6; 24:5). By using these exemptions to explain why they cannot attend, they call attention to the dinner. The *eschaton* will not arrive without struggle. In order to sit at the banquet table in the kingdom of heaven, one must value it above any other facet of life, and acting on this value will be a struggle of warlike proportions. The banquet therefore becomes a metaphor for victory in the battle on behalf of the kingdom of God. Those refusing to come to the dinner demonstrate that they recognize this point. They simply do not hold the kingdom in as high regard as their daily affairs, as noble as those affairs may be.

The metaphor continues. The rich and wealthy have no need to participate in a banquet. The poor in the nearby city and district, who need the protection and favor of a rich lord, jump at the chance to go. There is still room at the table, so the invitation goes out to those who have no relationship to the host, and thus neither the host nor these guests have anything to gain from each other. The invitation is a purely gracious act.

The lesson of the parable places Jesus' mission in a microcosm. The self-satisfied, self-sufficient, and self-righteous are welcomed into the kingdom, but their self-inflated importance will block their will to enter. Those knowing their spiritual destitution will enter the kingdom willingly, and the Gentiles, who have no legal claim or right to come and dine, will also be invited to fill the dining hall.

14:25-35 The cost of discipleship

The Gospel of Matthew (10:37-38) shows a shortened parallel of verses 25-27. At the core of both accounts is Q source material, which Luke expands. The expansion continues into verses 28-33, a section that has no parallels. Luke concludes with a form of the saying about salt (vv. 34-35), which appears in all three Synoptics.

The language in verse 26 is harsh. In a reflection of the Semitic convention to employ hyperbole in order to make a point, Luke uses the Greek verb *miseō*, a term meaning "detest" or "abhor." The lesson teaches that no earthly attachment to a person, place, or thing should keep us from following God. Discipleship requires singleness of purpose, and this purpose is to go beyond natural ties and allegiances for the sake of the kingdom. Doing so will not be easy (v. 27).

The image seems to switch in verses 28-33, but the purpose of this scene is closely aligned to the preceding material and, in fact, explains it. Constructing a major building or preparing for a military expedition requires a great deal of planning. An architect or a general must calculate losses and the gains and make a decision accordingly. Being a disciple demands at least as much time and consideration. Disciples must acknowledge what they must sacrifice in order to take up the cross (v. 33).

References to building a tower and marching into battle may have been drawn from the life experience of the day. Herod the Great launched major construction in Caesarea Maritima, Jericho, Jerusalem, and even in the desert. Each of these projects involved a tremendous amount of planning to organize both human and material resources. Likewise, there was a major dispute between Herod Antipas and King Aretas of Nabatea, based on the former's divorce of his first wife, who was a Nabatean princess, in order to marry Herod Philip's wife, Herodias. Ultimately, this dispute turned into a war, which ended when Rome intervened and forced King Aretas to give up his plans.

The whole lesson ends with the salt metaphor (vv. 34-35). In order for salt to lose its taste, it would have to cease being sodium chloride. Analogously, disciples who shrug off the cross cease being disciples of Christ.

15:1-32 Parables of the lost

At this point in the journey to Jerusalem, Luke has constructed a series of parables and lessons dealing with sinners and their chance for salvation.

Luke groups together three parables dealing with valuables lost and found. These par-

and children, brothers and sisters, and even his own life, he cannot be my disciple. [27]Whoever does not carry his own cross and come after me cannot be my disciple. [28]Which of you wishing to construct a tower does not first sit down and calculate the cost to see if there is enough for its completion? [29]Otherwise, after laying the foundation and finding himself unable to finish the work the onlookers should laugh at him [30]and say, 'This one began to build but did not have the resources to finish.' [31]Or what king marching into battle would not first sit down and decide whether with ten thousand troops he can successfully oppose another king advancing upon him with twenty thousand troops? [32]But if not, while he is still far away, he will send a delegation to ask for peace terms. [33]In the same way, everyone of you who does not renounce all his possessions cannot be my disciple.

The Simile of Salt

[34]"Salt is good, but if salt itself loses its taste, with what can its flavor be restored? [35]It is fit neither for the soil nor for the manure pile; it is thrown out. Whoever has ears to hear ought to hear."

CHAPTER 15

The Parable of the Lost Sheep

[1]The tax collectors and sinners were all drawing near to listen to him, [2]but the Pharisees and scribes began to complain, saying, "This man welcomes sinners and eats with them." [3]So to them he addressed this parable. [4]"What man among you having a hundred sheep and losing one of them would not leave the ninety-nine in the

continue

ables form a unit in which the central personage in each story line is the Christ figure, and the person or object lost is then seen as the sinner. Two of the parables, those of the lost coin and the prodigal son, are found only in Luke's Gospel.

desert and go after the lost one until he finds it? [5]And when he does find it, he sets it on his shoulders with great joy [6]and, upon his arrival home, he calls together his friends and neighbors and says to them, 'Rejoice with me because I have found my lost sheep.' [7]I tell you, in just the same way there will be more joy in heaven over one sinner who repents than over ninety-nine righteous people who have no need of repentance.

The Parable of the Lost Coin

[8]"Or what woman having ten coins and losing one would not light a lamp and sweep the house, searching carefully until she finds it? [9]And when she does find it, she calls together her friends and neighbors and says to them, 'Rejoice with me because I have found the coin that I lost.' [10]In just the same way, I tell you, there will be rejoicing among the angels of God over one sinner who repents."

continue

15:1-7 The parable of the lost sheep

Although this parable is Q material, Luke's introduction to it is different from Matthew 18:12-14. In Luke, Pharisees and scribes are grumbling about the tax collectors and sinners who gravitate toward Jesus. Their complaining leads into the parable of the lost sheep. The rhetorical question "What man among you . . .?" (v. 4) relies on the common sense of the listener to conclude that no one would leave a whole flock to go after one lost sheep. The ridiculousness of leaving ninety-nine sheep in the desert to find a stray defies the imagination, but such ridiculousness is the point of the parable. Nearly equally ridiculous is inviting neighbors and friends to celebrate the return of the stray.

God's love for his creatures is so strong that it includes even the sinners, something that self-righteous individuals have a hard time appreciating. The joy that spreads through heaven also strikes our human ears as over-

much, but it emphasizes the divine welcome given to the repentant sinner.

The Greek uses *anthrōpos* for "man" (v. 4) and thus is a gender-inclusive term. Often in the Holy Land, both in antiquity and now, shepherds are boys, girls, and women, an interesting perspective for the story considering that the shepherd is the Christ figure.

15:8-10 The parable of the lost coin

The Greek for "coin," *drachma*, was of the approximate value of a *denarius* and was worth about one day's wage for a laborer; the woman's diligent search, therefore, is certainly justified. When the object of the search, in this case a coin, is compared to the lost sheep in the previous parable, we can see an increase in the stakes. No matter how valuable one sheep is in earthly terms, it is not worth risking ninety-nine other sheep to find it. In this parable, however, the other nine coins are not placed in jeopardy as the woman seeks out the lost coin.

As with the parable of the yeast (13:20-21), the woman is the Christ figure, and her intense desire to find the lost coin is analogous to God's desire to find the lost sinner. Moreover, the parable says something about the value of the lost sinner in God's eyes. Here the mention of the rejoicing among the angels (v. 10) echoes the heavenly rejoicing found in the parable of the lost sheep (15:7). In both cases, such a conclusion keeps the eschatological focus of the message.

We read that a woman lights a lamp to sweep the house, a detail that gives evidence of the Syrian origins of Luke's Gospel. Unlike houses in the Judean Hills or even the semi-arid desert fringes of the south, which were constructed of comparatively lightweight limestone or sandstone, allowing for use of windows and other openings, houses on the Syrian plains and heights had a different building material and style altogether. In these areas the common building block was the very heavy, volcanic, black basalt stone. To support upper stories, the walls of these buildings had to be of solid construction and could not contain many, if any, windows. Consequently, interior living spaces were dark, and lighting a lamp would have been necessary, even in broad daylight.

15:11-32 The parable of the prodigal son

This parable has had a great influence on Western art, being depicted in drama, music, ballet, and painting.

The story opens with the younger son asking his father for his share of the inheritance. Of course, it is for the father to decide whether his son deserves it, not the son himself. By his action the younger son communicates that he does not view the inheritance as a gift bequeathed to him because of his father's good graces; rather, he sees it as his due.

According to ancient Jewish custom (Num 27:8-11; 36:7-9), an inheritance is the father's property, which, according to the custom of the day, the father gave to his sons, although he was not bound by any means to do so. When the younger son demands his share of the inheritance, therefore, he is asking the father for a part of the father's life. It is as if the son is requesting the father's very soul, an understanding emphasized by the Greek term for "property," *bios*, the same word used for "life" or "living" (v. 12). By his request, the son is indirectly demanding the father's own death. The father, however, instead of taking insult with his son's effrontery, gives him the inheritance.

The young son squanders the inheritance on "a life of dissipation" (v. 13). The idea is that the son's living is so extravagant, profligate, wasteful, and glitzy, that there is nothing of merit in any of it. Not only is the son jeopardizing his physical life by dangerous living, but the return of enjoyment on his investment is so meager that it makes the whole venture worthless.

To feed a pig, which represents everything reprehensible to every Jewish sensibility, would be a curse indeed. God-fearing Gentiles in the Lukan community would have been familiar enough with Jewish customs to know how low the young son descended. The son is absolutely alienated from the community. The

The Parable of the Lost Son

[11]Then he said, "A man had two sons, [12]and the younger son said to his father, 'Father, give me the share of your estate that should come to me.' So the father divided the property between them. [13]After a few days, the younger son collected all his belongings and set off to a distant country where he squandered his inheritance on a life of dissipation. [14]When he had freely spent everything, a severe famine struck that country, and he found himself in dire need. [15]So he hired himself out to one of the local citizens who sent him to his farm to tend the swine. [16]And he longed to eat his fill of the pods on which the swine fed, but nobody gave him any. [17]Coming to his senses he thought, 'How many of my father's hired workers have more than enough food to eat, but here am I, dying from hunger. [18]I shall get up and go to my father and I shall say to him, "Father, I have sinned against heaven and against you. [19]I no longer deserve to be called your son; treat me as you would treat one of your hired workers." ' [20]So he got up and went back to his father. While he was still a long way off, his father caught sight of him, and was filled with compassion. He ran to his son, embraced him and kissed him. [21]His son said to him, 'Father, I have sinned against heaven and against you; I no longer deserve to be called your son.' [22]But his father ordered his servants, 'Quickly bring the finest robe and put it on him; put a ring on his finger and sandals on his feet. [23]Take the fattened calf and slaughter it. Then let us celebrate with a feast, [24]because this son of mine was dead, and has come to life again; he was lost, and has been found.' Then the celebration began. [25]Now the older son had been out in the field and, on his way back, as he neared the house, he heard the sound of music and dancing. [26]He called one of the servants and asked what this might mean. [27]The servant said to him, 'Your brother has returned and your father has slaughtered the fattened calf because he has him back safe and sound.' [28]He became angry, and when he

continue

refused to enter the house, his father came out and pleaded with him. ²⁹He said to his father in reply, 'Look, all these years I served you and not once did I disobey your orders; yet you never gave me even a young goat to feast on with my friends. ³⁰But when your son returns who swallowed up your property with prostitutes, for him you slaughter the fattened calf.' ³¹He said to him, 'My son, you are here with me always; everything I have is yours. ³²But now we must celebrate and rejoice, because your brother was dead and has come to life again; he was lost and has been found.'"

continue

pods (Greek: *kerátion*) were probably from the carob tree and would be fit for human consumption (v. 16).

With verse 17 the audience is prepared for the next part, where the son acknowledges his sinfulness: "Father, I have sinned against heaven and against you; I no longer deserve to be called your son" (vv. 18b-19). Despite his egregiously bad behavior, he plans to ask for the status of a hired hand, which actually is how his father should have and could have treated him when he asked for the inheritance in the first place.

Father and son meet in verse 20, and the son begins his rehearsed speech, but he does not get to finish it. The father, so moved and filled with emotion at his son's return, does not hear a word he says. He cuts the son off in mid-sentence and tells the servants to prepare for a party, and he explains, "because this son of mine was dead, and has come to life again; he was lost and has been found" (v. 24). Because the son never has the opportunity to call himself a "hired hand," one cannot say that the father is refuting his son's assessment. Rather, we the audience can see that the father has always held this son in high regard and has never stopped loving him. The father's love

and generosity toward his lost, now found son so border on the ridiculous that his actions preclude his wayward son's expression of shame and guilt. We have here a loving father whose love exceeds all bounds.

This parable then switches focus to the elder brother (v. 25). By external measure, the elder brother has been obedient and respectful of the father, whom his younger brother has both insulted and grieved. The dialogue between the son and the father, however, challenges such an assumption of his filial relationship.

The elder brother, after citing off his own virtues, explodes in front of his father (vv. 29-30). The father, defending his own act of forgiveness, corrects the elder brother (v. 32). The father insists that the prodigal son is both a son to him and a brother to his other son. The one who has been alienated is now restored to the family.

The elder son is blind to his father's magnanimity. As an elder son, he has a duty to support the father in his decisions, a duty that he obviously shirks. The positions are reversed. Now it is the elder brother who insults and acts disrespectfully, while the younger son, by humbling himself, shows respect. In spite of this, the father still goes on loving, this time toward the elder son (v. 31). The father's forgiveness and charity maintain the ties of a loving relationship toward both his sons. As with all parables, this one turns to the listener, asking us to identify with either the younger son, the elder brother, or the father.

In each of the successive parables of the lost, that which is lost increases in value, from stray lamb, to a drachma, to a son. With such a progression, the worth of the sinner also increases in God's eyes, and the listener is left with the conclusion that God loves all as parents love their children. Furthermore, in the first two parables the shepherd and the woman are the Christ figure, respectively. In the parable of the prodigal son, however, it is not absolutely clear whether the father is Christ or God the Father, and this ambiguity, no doubt, is intentional.

16:1-13 The parable of the dishonest steward

This parable appears only in Luke's Gospel. That the steward is clever to the point of being crafty makes the fact that Jesus commends him difficult for us to appreciate.

Stewards made a living by collecting rents and debts for their masters and charging the debtors interest on the amount owed, which would then go to the stewards' coffers. Here the steward is shameless in the lengths he will go to maintain his position. He is not trying to hide anything from the rich man; indeed, he may even want his employer to find out about his altering the books. His hope is that his cleverness may win back the rich man's favor, and barring that outcome, he will at least have made some grateful constituents to take him in. The steward's audaciousness in achieving his ends calls attention to Jesus' lesson. Anyone of us would go to the greatest lengths, no matter how unsavory, to ensure a secure place in this world; how much more should we devote our attention to the world to come (v. 8).

Jesus names the problem in verse 9. The term "dishonest wealth" reflects the danger that inheres in worldly goods. Jesus warns the listener to use the wealth, but not to place any trust in it. Only trusting in God will lead to an eternal dwelling; everything else is counterfeit.

The narrative then discusses the conclusions one can draw from the parable by indirectly referring to the description of the steward (vv. 10-13). In verse 1 the steward is accused of "squandering" the master's property. The steward has mismanaged, perhaps through incompetence, the "very small matters" of this world, so there is no reason to trust him in the larger matters of the next one (v. 10). That lesson is turned toward the audience in verse 12. Trust is earned, it is not assumed. Those who deal loosely and unethically with others should not expect others to honor and trust them.

Verse 13 is a Q saying that also appears in Matthew 6:24. "Mammon" (v. 13), a Greek transliteration of the Aramaic word, means more than wealth and riches; it can signify anything of this world that one relies on: titles,

CHAPTER 16

The Parable of the Dishonest Steward

[1]Then he also said to his disciples, "A rich man had a steward who was reported to him for squandering his property. [2]He summoned him and said, 'What is this I hear about you? Prepare a full account of your stewardship, because you can no longer be my steward.' [3]The steward said to himself, 'What shall I do, now that my master is taking the position of steward away from me? I am not strong enough to dig and I am ashamed to beg. [4]I know what I shall do so that, when I am removed from the stewardship, they may welcome me into their homes.' [5]He called in his master's debtors one by one. To the first he said, 'How much do you owe my master?' [6]He replied, 'One hundred measures of olive oil.' He said to him, 'Here is your promissory note. Sit down and quickly write one for fifty.' [7]Then to another he said, 'And you, how much do you owe?' He replied, 'One hundred kors of wheat.' He said to him, 'Here is your promissory note; write one for eighty.' [8]And the master commended that dishonest steward for acting prudently.

Application of the Parable

"For the children of this world are more prudent in dealing with their own generation than are the children of light. [9]I tell you, make friends for yourselves with dishonest wealth, so that when it fails, you will be welcomed into eternal dwellings. [10]The person who is trustworthy in very small matters is also trustworthy in great ones; and the person who is dishonest in very small matters is also dishonest in great ones. [11]If, therefore, you are not trustworthy with dishonest wealth, who will trust you with true wealth?

continue

positions, privileges, and honors. To be sure, wealth is tied up with many of these perquisites, but mammon is anything which takes our attention away from God, the true source of life.

¹²If you are not trustworthy with what belongs to another, who will give you what is yours? ¹³No servant can serve two masters. He will either hate one and love the other, or be devoted to one and despise the other. You cannot serve God and mammon."

A Saying against the Pharisees

¹⁴The Pharisees, who loved money, heard all these things and sneered at him. ¹⁵And he said to them, "You justify yourselves in the sight of others, but God knows your hearts; for what is of human esteem is an abomination in the sight of God.

Sayings about the Law

¹⁶"The law and the prophets lasted until John; but from then on the kingdom of God is proclaimed, and everyone who enters does so with violence. ¹⁷It is easier for heaven and earth to pass away than for the smallest part of a letter of the law to become invalid.

Sayings about Divorce

¹⁸"Everyone who divorces his wife and marries another commits adultery, and the one who marries a woman divorced from her husband commits adultery.

The Parable of the Rich Man and Lazarus

¹⁹"There was a rich man who dressed in purple garments and fine linen and dined sumptuously

continue

16:14-15 Encounter with the Pharisees

Luke alone features this reproof, which, with the notice that this particular group of Pharisees "loved money" (v. 14), is tied to the warning about wealth above. Jesus directs the criticism at the human desire for self-justification and public praise. The performance of good deeds, then, goes only as far as human acclaim. In such a case, people will never do an act that may be good but unpopular.

16:16-18 Sayings on the Law and divorce

The "law" in this passage refers to the Mosaic Law, the Jewish religious and cultic legislation, and reflects the context from which the Christian movement emerged. The evangelists and other New Testament writers interpreted the Old Testament, comprised of books both in Hebrew and Greek, as the precursor to the revelation of Christ. Now the "kingdom of God is proclaimed," but the ability to move into a new way of viewing one's relationship with God is not easy; hence "everyone who enters does so with violence" (v. 16). Jewish Christians found that the change from the Mosaic Law to Christ required a major shift in focus, and Gentile Christians, at first not welcome unless they had undergone conversion to Judaism (see Acts 10; 15), put themselves at risk with their pagan neighbors. Luke's Gospel stresses Christ as the ultimate arbiter of any interpretation of the Law (v. 17); in that sense, the law will not pass away, as the next saying demonstrates (v. 18).

Luke and Mark agree against Matthew in their readings on the prohibition of divorce. While Matthew sees unchastity as a mitigating circumstance for dissolving the marriage (see Matt 19:9; Mark 10:11-12), Luke's version of divorce legislation (v. 18) serves as an example of how the Law has lost its validity. According to the Mosaic teaching, a man could divorce his wife by simply signing a statement of dismissal; the woman had no similar option (Deut 24:1-4). Consequently, the woman and her children would be left to fend for themselves by begging and prostitution. Jesus nullifies this legislation by declaring that no one can divorce, and thereby demonstrates that the law and the prophets ended with John (v. 16).

16:19-31 The rich man and Lazarus

This parable appears only in Luke and reflects the evangelist's overriding concern for the poor and for social justice. In the tradition this is also known as the story of Dives and Lazarus, the former name stemming from the Latin *dives*, meaning "rich person." It is one of the best known of all Gospel stories, even prompting Ralph Vaughan Williams to compose a musical score based on this story. The name "Lazarus" itself is the Greek transliteration of the Hebrew abbreviation "Eleazar," a name that means "God has helped." Thematically, it is tied to the saying about God and mammon in 16:13.

The "rich man" of the parable stands in contrast to the **reverence for all human beings** taught by the Second Vatican Council. According to *Gaudium et Spes* "everybody should look upon his or her neighbor (without any exception) as another self, bearing in mind especially their neighbor's life and the means needed for a dignified way of life" (27). Catholic social teaching recognizes that the way societies are organized often makes it hard to treat one's neighbor with dignity and respect. Consequently believers are challenged to change laws, policies, procedures, and social attitudes, to promote the dignity and respect of every human being.

The information concerning the rich man's clothing (v. 19) indicates that he is not simply well off—he is excessively wealthy. Purple dye was a costly commodity that very few people even among the rich could afford. These details heighten the contrast between the rich man and Lazarus, who not only has sores that dogs would lick but who even lacks the simplest garment to cover those sores. That Lazarus keeps company with dogs accentuates his dismal state, since dogs were considered filthy, undesirable animals.

Luke illustrates the theme of the great reversal in this parable, first outlined in the *Magnificat* (see Luke 1:46-55). In the parable the hungry are literally "filled with good things," while the rich are "sent away empty" (1:53). The dialogue between Abraham and the rich man amply describes the new state of things.

each day. ²⁰And lying at his door was a poor man named Lazarus, covered with sores, ²¹who would gladly have eaten his fill of the scraps that fell from the rich man's table. Dogs even used to come and lick his sores. ²²When the poor man died, he was carried away by angels to the bosom of Abraham. The rich man also died and was buried, ²³and from the netherworld, where he was in torment, he raised his eyes and saw Abraham far off and Lazarus at his side. ²⁴And he cried out, 'Father Abraham, have pity on me. Send Lazarus to dip the tip of his finger in water and cool my tongue, for I am suffering torment in these flames.' ²⁵Abraham replied, 'My child, remember that you received what was good during your lifetime while Lazarus likewise received what was bad; but now he is comforted here, whereas you are tormented. ²⁶Moreover, between us and you a great chasm is established to prevent anyone from crossing who might wish to go from our side to yours or from your side to ours.' ²⁷He said, 'Then I beg you, father, send him to my father's house, ²⁸for I have five brothers, so that he may warn them, lest they too come to this place of torment.' ²⁹But Abraham replied, 'They have Moses and the prophets. Let them listen to them.' ³⁰He said, 'Oh no, father Abraham, but if someone from the dead goes to them, they will repent.' ³¹Then Abraham said, 'If they will not listen to Moses and the prophets, neither will they be persuaded if someone should rise from the dead.'"

We know that the rich man cannot claim ignorance of the fact that someone hungry is outside his door, for he refers to Lazarus by name (v. 24). There is even an arrogant tone in his request: he does not ask Abraham for the favor but requests that Abraham command Lazarus to come down and refresh him. Most likely he treated Lazarus in a similar fashion when they both were alive.

Abraham, in his reply, ensures that the rich man knows exactly why he is where he is so that neither the rich man, now suffering the flames of the netherworld, nor the audience can conclude that he is a victim of a great misfortune. No, the rich man's lack of charity and responsibility put him there; indeed, the rich man's great sin of omission fashioned the chasm between the two. We are forced to wonder why the chasm cannot be crossed. The answer says a great deal about salvation and damnation.

The lesson is not that God is a God of damnation and punishment, inasmuch as it gives us an example of how much of a role we play in our salvation. The rich man was oblivious to the needs of those around him while he was alive, and now that he is dead, he is still oblivious, as his call for Lazarus's services suggests. Herein lies the danger of wealth that Jesus always preaches: power and wealth blind us to the kingdom of God in this life and in the next. If we are not wide-eyed to the kingdom and its demands now, as Moses and the prophets tell us to be (v. 31), we will not be sensitive to seeing the kingdom after we die. The great irony in the story is that the rich man needs Lazarus in order to be saved. Had he paid attention to Lazarus begging for table scraps at the door of his house, the rich man would not be in the predicament he is in now.

The last verse of the parable, of course, is a reference to Jesus' own resurrection.

EXPLORING LESSON TWO

1. What do Jesus' instructions concerning both guests and hosts at a dinner party teach us about the kingdom of God (14:7-14)? (See Sir 32:1-2.)

_____

_____

_____

_____

2. In providing excuses for ignoring God's call to feast in the kingdom, how different or similar are worldly concerns today (14:15-24)?

_____

_____

_____

_____

3. What lies at the heart of Jesus' insistence that we must "hate" members of our family if we are to come to him (14:25-35)? (See Luke 9:59-62; 1 Kgs 19:19-21; Ps 27:10.)

_____

_____

_____

_____

4. a) In Luke 15:1-32, Jesus tells three parables about the joy in the kingdom of God at finding those who have been lost. When have you experienced joy in being reunited with someone or something that had been lost?

_____

_____

_____

_____

   b) Which character in the parable of the lost son (15:11-32) do you have the most questions about (the father, the younger son, the elder son, the mother who is not mentioned)? What more would you like to know about that character?

_____

_____

_____

_____

5. The parable of the dishonest steward (16:1-9) is considered one of Jesus' most difficult to appreciate. What positive message can you find in the parable?

6. What matters large or small has God entrusted into your care (16:10-13)?

7. What pressures do married couples face that bring so much stress on marriage commitments today (16:16-18)?

8. Where in your daily life have you encountered modern-day "Lazaruses" (16:19-31)? How can we best respond to their needs?

CLOSING PRAYER

Prayer

"When you hold a banquet, invite the poor, the crippled, the lame, the blind; blessed indeed will you be because of their inability to repay you." (Luke 14:13-14)

O God, remind us that you are the host who has invited us to the banquet of your kingdom. You see our poverty and blindness and welcome us to your table. We pause to thank you for your generosity.

We ask you also to warm our hearts toward those whose poverty separates us from them. We pray for the desire to open our hearts and tables more widely, especially in these ways . . .

LESSON THREE

Luke 17–19

Begin your personal study and group discussion with a simple and sincere prayer such as:

Prayer

God of all goodness, open my heart to hear you speak through the Gospel of Luke. Help me to journey faithfully toward Jerusalem with Jesus.

Read the Bible text of Luke 17–19 found in the outside columns of pages 42–53, highlighting what stands out to you.

Read the accompanying commentary to add to your understanding.

Respond to the questions on pages 54–55, Exploring Lesson Three.

The closing prayer on page 56 is for your personal use and may be used at the end of group discussion.

CHAPTER 17

Temptations to Sin

¹He said to his disciples, "Things that cause sin will inevitably occur, but woe to the person through whom they occur. ²It would be better for him if a millstone were put around his neck and he be thrown into the sea than for him to cause one of these little ones to sin. ³Be on your guard! If your brother sins, rebuke him; and if he repents, forgive him. ⁴And if he wrongs you seven times in one day and returns to you seven times saying, 'I am sorry,' you should forgive him."

Saying of Faith

⁵And the apostles said to the Lord, "Increase our faith." ⁶The Lord replied, "If you have faith the size of a mustard seed, you would say to [this] mulberry tree, 'Be uprooted and planted in the sea,' and it would obey you.

Attitude of a Servant

⁷"Who among you would say to your servant who has just come in from plowing or tending sheep in the field, 'Come here immediately and

continue

This mercy and tenderness, however, are not to be regarded as permission for further injury. Those who sin are to be rebuked, and if sinners repent, they are to be forgiven. The Gospel sees rebuke and forgiveness as a means of achieving both personal salvation and social justice. On the other hand, lest repentance and forgiveness be exercised on a quid pro quo basis, the saying continues with the proviso that because sins or even the same sin will occur numerous times, it must be forgiven each time the sinner repents. We are to imitate divine forgiveness in its limitlessness.

This passage addresses only how to deal with sinful behavior within the church community, but for Luke, mercy extends to those outside the community as well (see Luke 6:27-36).

17:1-4 Temptations to sin

The journey to Jerusalem continues with further instruction along the way.

Each Synoptic Gospel has a variation of the warning against giving offense. Verses 3-4 parallel Matthew 18:15, thereby making them Q material. Luke injects a note of reality in verse 1b: as long as there is a believing community, there will be scandals. As great a sin as it is to lead one into temptation, it is far greater to do so to a "little one" (v. 2). Millstones, even one for household use, were heavy and expensive. The punishment suggested is severe indeed.

Where there is sin, there must be forgiveness, and Luke gracefully connects the two. We have another example of the mercy and tenderness that are so much a part of the third Gospel.

17:5-6 Saying on faith

Once again, faith is compared to a mustard seed (see Luke 13:19), but the example switches to a sycamine tree (*morus nigra*; read "mulberry" in the text), a large tree with clustered berries. Both Matthew and Luke use the hyperbole from Q to make their point that nothing is impossible to the person who has faith. Matthew's phrase, however, refers to moving a mountain, which most scholars believe to be the original version.

17:7-10 The attitude of a servant

This piece on servants occurs only in Luke.

The social world of the Gospel is particularly evident in this passage dealing with masters and slaves. The lesson is that Christians should not expect praise and honor for performing those duties that they are obligated to perform. Moreover, the saying counters the thought that salvation can be gained on human merit alone and without God's grace. If our own deeds render us unprofitable servants, we have no other recourse for salvation than to depend on the divine initiative.

17:11-19 The cleansing of ten lepers

The prescription to the lepers to show themselves to the priests is found in Leviticus 14:2-9.

The most common route for Jews in Galilee to go to Jerusalem was through the Jordan Valley. Although cutting down through Samaria was not impossible, most Jews preferred to avoid Samaritan territory (see Luke 9:52). Did Jesus ever set foot in Samaria? Verse 11 can be translated "through the region between Samaria and Galilee." This passage is solely Lukan material and shows Luke's proclivity to highlight the faith of the social outcast over that of the established insider. Both Jews (Galileans) and Samaritans compose this group of

take your place at table'? [8]Would he not rather say to him, 'Prepare something for me to eat. Put on your apron and wait on me while I eat and drink. You may eat and drink when I am finished'? [9]Is he grateful to that servant because he did what was commanded? [10]So should it be with you. When you have done all you have been commanded, say, 'We are unprofitable servants; we have done what we were obliged to do.'"

The Cleansing of Ten Lepers

[11]As he continued his journey to Jerusalem, he traveled through Samaria and Galilee. [12]As he was entering a village, ten lepers met [him]. They stood at a distance from him [13]and raised their

continue

lepers; both are society's outcasts, and therefore they associate with each other.

Luke's eschatological vision comes into focus with the emphasis on faith in verse 19. Jesus instructs the Samaritan leper, not that his

The Grateful Samaritan

The story of the Good Samaritan is so much a part of our culture that we talk about "being a Good Samaritan" and we pass "Good Samaritan laws" to protect those who help others in an emergency. Maybe we can begin to bring another Samaritan into our consciousness—the grateful Samaritan.

When Jesus was met by ten lepers as he was passing through Samaria, we are told the lepers stood at a distance and "raised their voice . . . 'Jesus, Master! Have pity on us!'" Collectively they asked for attention and mercy. Collectively they were cleansed. However, only one of them, a Samaritan, returned to thank Jesus. Why?

First, the Samaritan leper realized he had been healed. Perhaps we can think about times when we suddenly felt stronger after a bout of the flu, or one day realized that some sadness had lifted. Gratitude begins when we become aware of what is happening in our lives and how we are being changed.

Second, the leper knew that his healing was not his own doing. If we fail to recognize that God is the source of our healing, cleansing, new spirit, or success, then we may miss the gift of felt gratitude. Gratitude is the natural response to a God who makes us whole.

Finally, the leper knew that he was shunned not only because of a skin condition but because he was a Samaritan. When Jesus took notice of him, it changed his perception of himself as an outsider. Gratitude flowed from his sense of worth and dignity as a person, restored to him by Jesus' acceptance.

voice, saying, "Jesus, Master! Have pity on us!" ¹⁴And when he saw them, he said, "Go show yourselves to the priests." As they were going they were cleansed. ¹⁵And one of them, realizing he had been healed, returned, glorifying God in a loud voice; ¹⁶and he fell at the feet of Jesus and thanked him. He was a Samaritan. ¹⁷Jesus said in reply, "Ten were cleansed, were they not? Where are the other nine? ¹⁸Has none but this foreigner returned to give thanks to God?" ¹⁹Then he said to him, "Stand up and go; your faith has saved you."

The Coming of the Kingdom of God

²⁰Asked by the Pharisees when the kingdom of God would come, he said in reply, "The coming of the kingdom of God cannot be observed, ²¹and no one will announce, 'Look, here it is,' or, 'There it is.' For behold, the kingdom of God is among you."

The Day of the Son of Man

²²Then he said to his disciples, "The days will come when you will long to see one of the days of the Son of Man, but you will not see it. ²³There will be those who will say to you, 'Look, there he is,' [or] 'Look, here he is.' Do not go off, do not run in pursuit. ²⁴For just as lightning flashes and lights up the sky from one side to the other, so will the Son of Man be [in his day]. ²⁵But first he must suffer greatly and be rejected by this generation. ²⁶As it was in the days of Noah, so it will be in the days of the Son of Man; ²⁷they were eating and drinking, marrying and giving in marriage up to the day that Noah entered the ark, and the flood came and destroyed them all. ²⁸Similarly, as it was in the days of Lot: they were eating, drinking, buying, selling, planting, building; ²⁹on the day when Lot left Sodom, fire and brimstone rained from the sky to destroy them all. ³⁰So it will be on the day the Son of Man is revealed. ³¹On that day, a person who is on the housetop and whose belongings are in the house must not go down to get them, and likewise a person in the

continue

faith has cured him, but that his faith has "saved" him. The leper is not only saved from his leprosy but gains eternal salvation—all from faith. The connection of faith with salvation occurs throughout Luke's Gospel, as we have seen with the woman in the house of Simon the Pharisee (7:50), the cure of the hemorrhaging woman (8:48), and even at the cross (23:43).

17:20-37 The coming of the kingdom and the Son of Man

In verses 20-21 Luke expresses a realized eschatology that supports the vision displayed in the dialogue with the Samaritan leper above. Indeed, the last phrase in verse 21 seems Johannine in its language as it underscores an *eschaton* already present.

The tone and theme switch suddenly to a future-oriented eschatology in verse 22. The opening words of this verse in Greek, which the English translation expresses, indicate a reversal of thought. In this first encounter with Lukan apocalyptic writing, the reading draws a parallel between sudden acts of destruction in the Old Testament and the Son of Man's impending arrival on the earth. Although found far more often in Ezekiel than in Daniel, the latter's use of "Son of Man" has greater bearing on the synoptic understanding of this term, an understanding that Luke shares. The heavily apocalyptic material in Daniel (see Dan 7:13; 8:15-17) is reflected in verse 22 and also figures prominently in the book of Revelation.

Luke includes a warning about following false prophets (as do the parallels in Mark and Matthew), but he also connects the coming of the eschaton with the fate awaiting Jesus in Jerusalem (v. 25). Furthermore, Luke builds a sense of urgency by relating Lot's escape from the explosive conflagration that destroyed Sodom; people should be vigilant and anxious. This sense of urgency also has a social justice theme, for injustice and oppression were the reasons for Sodom's obliteration (see Isa 1:9-16; Ezek 16:49-52). Any desire to hold on to the present is discouraged, and Lot's wife stands as an example of what might happen to the one who tarries. Those who make no permanent claims to this life will always be ready for the eschaton (v. 31).

To separate Jesus' words from the Gospel writer's is always extremely difficult. In this passage it is impossible. Verse 31 appears to be a prediction after the fact. Josephus describes the sudden arrival of the Romans at the gates of Jerusalem during the First Jewish Revolt (A.D. 66–70; J.W. 5.2.3]. Few if any were able to escape the destruction and massacre. The early Christians most likely interpreted the Jewish rebellion and the destruction of Jerusalem with its splendid temple as the fulfillment of Jesus' words, even as those words were mixed into their experiences of the catastrophe. What we have here is an amalgam of Q material, oral tradition, memory, and Lukan editing. (See Luke 21:20-24.)

One cannot take every passage of Scripture literally and apart from a larger theological context. Nowhere is this truer than in apocalyptic literature. Readers should be on guard against determining the saved, the damned, and the rapture by reading this material. Verse 37, in encouraging us to read the signs of the times, advises us to keep the whole Christian tradition in focus as we interpret those signs. And what are the signs? Jesus does not say, and this point is the essential part of the apocalyptic message.

Christians are to concern themselves with doing the will of God, for which Jesus has given his disciples abundant examples: taking care of the poor, trusting in God alone, and forgiving enemies. We are not to waste time trying to predict the future. The paradoxical presentation of the kingdom as already present (v. 21) and not yet here (v. 30) expresses its true reality. The kingdom will be manifested in living the life of Christ.

18:1-8 The parable of the persistent widow

Situating this pericope after the apocalyptic passage regarding the Son of Man offers the believer the proper way to maintain vigilance for the parousia, or second coming. With

field must not return to what was left behind. ³²Remember the wife of Lot. ³³Whoever seeks to preserve his life will lose it, but whoever loses it will save it. ³⁴I tell you, on that night there will be two people in one bed; one will be taken, the other left. ³⁵And there will be two women grinding meal together; one will be taken, the other left." [³⁶] ³⁷They said to him in reply, "Where, Lord?" He said to them, "Where the body is, there also the vultures will gather."

CHAPTER 18

The Parable of the Persistent Widow

¹Then he told them a parable about the necessity for them to pray always without becoming weary. He said, ²"There was a judge in a certain town who neither feared God nor respected any human being. ³And a widow in that town used to come to him and say, 'Render a just decision for me against my adversary.' ⁴For a long time the judge was unwilling, but eventually he thought, 'While it is true that I neither fear God nor respect any human being, ⁵because this widow keeps bothering me I shall deliver a just decision for her lest she finally come and strike me.' " ⁶The Lord said, "Pay attention to what the dishonest judge says. ⁷Will not God then secure the rights of his chosen ones who call out to him day and night? Will he be slow to answer them? ⁸I tell you, he will see to it that justice is done for them speedily. But when the Son of Man comes, will he find faith on earth?"

continue

prayer and praying mentioned over thirty times in Luke's Gospel and the Acts of the Apostles, the parable of the persistent widow highlights this central feature of Luke's Gospel by emphasizing the necessity and efficacy of constant prayer. Moreover, because widows and orphans were to be special recipients of charity according to Jewish law (Deut 24:17-22), the early Christians would have been particularly attentive to the teaching.

The Parable of the Pharisee and the Tax Collector

⁹He then addressed this parable to those who were convinced of their own righteousness and despised everyone else. ¹⁰"Two people went up to the temple area to pray; one was a Pharisee and the other was a tax collector. ¹¹The Pharisee took up his position and spoke this prayer to himself, 'O God, I thank you that I am not like the rest of humanity—greedy, dishonest, adulterous—or even like this tax collector. ¹²I fast twice a week, and I pay tithes on my whole income.' ¹³But the tax collector stood off at a distance and would not even raise his eyes to heaven but beat his breast and prayed, 'O God, be merciful to me a sinner.' ¹⁴I tell you, the latter went home justified, not the former; for everyone who exalts himself will be humbled, and the one who humbles himself will be exalted."

continue

The story appears only in Luke, and there are at least two ways to read it. The first is to see the unjust judge as the protagonist bearing the lesson for the reader. Similar to the literary style found in the parable of the dishonest steward (16:1-8), the intent of the teaching comes through the comparison of the greater: As an unjust judge grants a petition solely for self-serving purposes, how much more will a loving God grant the desires of his beloved petitioner.

A second, feminist interpretation, on the other hand, sees the widow as the protagonist and thus the vehicle for the lesson. In this case, she, in her weakness, becomes the Christ figure who combats evil and injustice on behalf of the poor and neglected. She is unstinting in her efforts, and the unjust judge, the symbol of oppression, is clearly afraid of her, as seen from the Greek verb *hypōpiazō* for "strike" (v. 5), which means to "treat roughly, maltreat, strike under the eye." Here, too, the intent of the teaching surfaces through analogy: As persis-

tent as a widow is to secure her rights, so is God in securing the rights of those petitioning him.

The reference to the Son of Man (v. 8) brings the parable in line with the teaching on the last days (17:22-37): Pray constantly while living and working for the kingdom of God.

18:9-14 The parable of the Pharisee and the tax collector

This parable, also found only in Luke, continues the theme on prayer. Whereas the parable of the persistent widow (18:1-8) shows the necessity of constant prayer, the parable of the Pharisee and the tax collector displays the proper comportment for prayer.

No doubt the Pharisee does everything he says he does. Fasting and tithing are not only good things to do, but the former is also proclaimed by the prophets while the latter is required by the Law (see Deut 14:22-29). The purpose of the parable is not to discourage religious and pious practice; rather, its function is to call into question the reasons why people take on devotional works. The Pharisee gives the reasons for deeds: they are to justify himself in the world's eyes as well as in the eyes of God. Luke underscores this point in verse 9.

In contrast, the tax collector does nothing pious that we know of. In fact, as a tax collector, it would be most surprising if he ever did anything good for anyone. During the Roman occupation, tax collectors were not only traitors to their own people but also extortionists feeding off their compatriots. Furthermore, their dealing with the pagan Romans made them ritually impure, thereby excommunicating themselves from their fellow Jews. Compared with the dedicated, devoted Pharisee, a tax collector would never be considered honest, pious, or holy. Unlike the Pharisee, however, the tax collector knows his sinfulness. He pleads for mercy and demonstrates his need for God. The Pharisee, on the other hand, in singing his own praises, makes God his beneficiary. That the tax collector leaves justified was as shocking to the first-century audience as it is to us. So important is this parable that it sets the tone for those participating in the passion and crucifixion (see 23:48).

18:15-17 Access to the kingdom

This passage stresses that the people brought infants to Jesus, whereas the parallels in Mark and Matthew read only that children came. The mention of infants gives a glimpse of the sociological structure in the ancient world. Conversions were never individualistic or isolated events. If the master or mistress of the household became a follower of Christ, everyone in the extended family and even the slaves did as well. In the Acts of the Apostles we read similar accounts regarding baptism (Acts 16:15, 33; 18:8). Luke's reading could very well reflect and suggest the practice of infant baptism in the early church.

Society today often presents Christianity as a childish, trivial, or trite matter and will use passages like this one to justify doing so. To "accept the kingdom of God like a child," however, means to receive the kingdom of God with an open guilelessness to the gift that God offers, something that requires a healthy maturity. In this case, the tax collector in the preceding passage (18:9-14) is the perfect example of open guilelessness.

18:18-23 The rich official

Although in their respective versions of the story, both Matthew and Mark simply state that a man comes up to Jesus, Luke specifies that the one asking the question is a ruler. Thus Luke informs the reader that the individual is not only rich but also powerful, an important point for the story.

The ruler's fault is one of complacency, and in this regard he is similar to the Pharisee in 18:9-14. When he calls Jesus "Good teacher" (v. 18), Jesus responds in a sharp tone, because he can see through the unctuous language. The ruler hopes that by flattery he can increase in stature to gain eternal life. Jesus continues with listing the prescriptions of the Decalogue. These statutes should recall the whole Exodus experience, in which the people struggle between their ever present faithlessness and their

Saying on Children and the Kingdom

[15]People were bringing even infants to him that he might touch them, and when the disciples saw this, they rebuked them. [16]Jesus, however, called the children to himself and said, "Let the children come to me and do not prevent them; for the kingdom of God belongs to such as these. [17]Amen, I say to you, whoever does not accept the kingdom of God like a child will not enter it."

The Rich Official

[18]An official asked him this question, "Good teacher, what must I do to inherit eternal life?" [19]Jesus answered him, "Why do you call me good? No one is good but God alone. [20]You know the commandments, 'You shall not commit adultery; you shall not kill; you shall not steal; you shall not bear false witness; honor your father and your mother.'" [21]And he replied, "All of these I have observed from my youth." [22]When Jesus heard this he said to him, "There is still one thing left for you: sell all that you have and distribute it to the poor, and you will have a treasure in heaven. Then come, follow me." [23]But when he heard this he became quite sad, for he was very rich.

continue

eventual trust in God. The ruler's answer that he has observed all the commandments from his youth demonstrates that he has completely forgotten that covenantal relationship expressed by trust in God.

Jesus concludes by entering the ruler's mind-set. The first half of the answer would catch the man's attention, "There is still one thing left for you . . ." (v. 22a). The ruler can handle the challenge; by his wits he has already accumulated wealth and power. Then comes the surprise: "sell all that you have and distribute it to the poor . . . come follow me" (v. 22b). The man's sadness results from a double realization. The first is that he must surrender everything of worth in his life, and the second follows, namely, that everything he thought

On Riches and Renunciation

²⁴Jesus looked at him [now sad] and said, "How hard it is for those who have wealth to enter the kingdom of God! ²⁵For it is easier for a camel to pass through the eye of a needle than for a rich person to enter the kingdom of God." ²⁶Those who heard this said, "Then who can be saved?" ²⁷And he said, "What is impossible for human beings is possible for God." ²⁸Then Peter said, "We have given up our possessions and followed you." ²⁹He said to them, "Amen, I say to you, there is no one who has given up house or wife or brothers or parents or children for the sake of the kingdom of God ³⁰who will not receive [back] an overabundant return in this present age and eternal life in the age to come."

The Third Prediction of the Passion

³¹Then he took the Twelve aside and said to them, "Behold, we are going up to Jerusalem and everything written by the prophets about the Son of Man will be fulfilled. ³²He will be handed over

continue

was of great value both in this life and the next is actually worthless. His life from his youth has been an act of faithlessness. To inherit eternal life, he must stop trusting in what he has trusted and place his trust in God.

18:24-30 On entering the kingdom of God

The dialogue with the rich official prompts Jesus' comment on the ease of a camel going through the eye of a needle, one of the most challenging verses in the Gospel (v. 25). The response from the crowd is certainly understandable: "Then who can be saved?" (v. 26).

A long-standing interpretation of this passage is that there was in Jerusalem a gate called the "Eye of the Needle," which required a cargo-laden camel to rest on all four legs and crawl through the door in order to enter the city. There is no evidence anywhere in the Mideast, however, of any gate called the "Eye of

the Needle." In addition, camels are unable to crawl. Jesus is using a form of hyperbole that is a natural part of Semitic speech.

The lesson that arises from this encounter with the ruler is similar to the one taught in the parable of the dishonest steward (16:1-13), where trusting in one's own wealth and accomplishments instead of in God makes salvation difficult if not impossible. In both cases the responsibility for accepting salvation falls on us. Those who place all hope in their own accomplishments will never be open to God's mercy, simply because they have let worldly values blind themselves to it. Since power and wealth are idols, and seductive ones at that, the ruler in the story and others like him cannot even see the way into the kingdom, let alone enter it. In this sense, it is easier for a camel to pass through a needle's eye.

Peter, sensing the meaning of Jesus' hyperbolic example, responds in verse 28. His statement implies that he is looking for an answer as to whether he and the other disciples are saved or not. Jesus does not answer directly; rather, his reply is addressed in the third person (vv. 29-30). Jesus' statement reflects a realized eschatology as well as a future one. Forsaking worldly comfort has a present reward, yet the reward is not fully realized until one reaches eternal life. Unlike the Markan parallel, which speaks of persecutions along with the rewards (Mark 10:30), Luke does not mention such hardships. Because the next passage contains the third prediction of the passion, Luke avoids the redundancy by not including the sobering fact here.

This passage has been used over the centuries as a rationale for religious life.

18:31-34 The third prediction of the passion

Being a disciple has its rewards, but it also has difficulties, as Jesus reminds his band of followers with this third, final, and most vivid prediction of his passion (see 9:22, 44-45; but also 17:25).

Although both Matthew and Mark feature parallels to this passage, only Luke contains information about the prophets (v. 31) and the Twelve's inability to understand what Jesus is saying (v. 34).

18:35-43 The blind beggar of Jericho

Jesus is relentlessly pursuing his intent as described in 9:51. In going from Galilee to Jerusalem through the Jordan Valley, one would turn west at Jericho in order to take the Wadi Qelt road up into the Judean mountains. Jericho, an oasis and a prosperous city in Judea, was also the locale of Herod the Great's winter palace. These facts serve to accentuate the beggar's lowly social position.

All three synoptic accounts contain this story, but only Mark gives the blind man a name (Bartimaeus; see Mark 10:46). Comparisons are very important here. This blind man can "see" Jesus is the Messiah, whereas the Twelve cannot understand what he is saying (v. 34). This paradox fits well within the Gospel tradition, where the blind usually "see," while those who "see" are actually blind.

The beggar uses one of the earliest Christian titles applied to Christ, "Son of David" (v. 38), a title that rarely appears in Luke (see 3:31; 20:41). Jesus hears the distressful cry despite the commotion of the crowd and their efforts to silence the man. Jesus could have walked to the man, but he commands that the beggar be brought to him (v. 40). Among religious people of the time, physical disability was linked to sinfulness. By having the crowd lead the blind man to him, Jesus induces them to take responsibility for healing him, thereby redefining both suffering and sin. Jesus does not assume that the beggar wants to see; rather, he asks him to explicitly state his need (v. 41). Of course, the beggar requests sight, because he knows that Jesus can grant it, and by this action he demonstrates his faith. Hence Jesus can say, "Your faith has saved you" (v. 42). In true Lukan fashion, in the end everyone—beggar and crowd—glorifies God.

19:1-10 Zacchaeus the tax collector

This passage appears only in Luke and concludes what many scholars have called the

to the Gentiles and he will be mocked and insulted and spat upon; ³³and after they have scourged him they will kill him, but on the third day he will rise." ³⁴But they understood nothing of this; the word remained hidden from them and they failed to comprehend what he said.

The Healing of the Blind Beggar

³⁵Now as he approached Jericho a blind man was sitting by the roadside begging, ³⁶and hearing a crowd going by, he inquired what was happening. ³⁷They told him, "Jesus of Nazareth is passing by." ³⁸He shouted, "Jesus, Son of David, have pity on me!" ³⁹The people walking in front rebuked him, telling him to be silent, but he kept calling out all the more, "Son of David, have pity on me!" ⁴⁰Then Jesus stopped and ordered that he be brought to him; and when he came near, Jesus asked him, ⁴¹"What do you want me to do for you?" He replied, "Lord, please let me see." ⁴²Jesus told him, "Have sight; your faith has saved you." ⁴³He immediately received his sight and followed him, giving glory to God. When they saw this, all the people gave praise to God.

CHAPTER 19

Zacchaeus the Tax Collector

¹He came to Jericho and intended to pass through the town. ²Now a man there named

continue

"Lukan Gospel of the Outcast" (15:1–19:10). Its singular character lies in the fact that Luke, who devotes the whole tone of his Gospel toward embracing the poor and lowly, includes this passage, which focuses on the salvation of the rich and powerful. Unlike the rich official in 18:18-23, Zacchaeus does not depend on his wealth and status but on God's loving mercy to gain entry into the kingdom.

Tax collecting was a lucrative business. Romans used to sell the office to the highest

Zacchaeus, who was a chief tax collector and also a wealthy man, ³was seeking to see who Jesus was; but he could not see him because of the crowd, for he was short in stature. ⁴So he ran ahead and climbed a sycamore tree in order to see Jesus, who was about to pass that way. ⁵When he reached the place, Jesus looked up and said to him, "Zacchaeus, come down quickly, for today I must stay at your house." ⁶And he came down quickly and received him with joy. ⁷When they all saw this, they began to grumble, saying, "He has gone to stay at the house of a sinner." ⁸But Zacchaeus stood there and said to the Lord, "Behold, half of my possessions, Lord, I shall give to the poor, and if I have extorted anything from anyone I shall repay it four times over." ⁹And Jesus said to him, "Today salvation has come to this house because this man too is a descendant of Abraham. ¹⁰For the Son of Man has come to seek and to save what was lost."

The Parable of the Ten Gold Coins

¹¹While they were listening to him speak, he proceeded to tell a parable because he was near Jerusalem and they thought that the kingdom of God would appear there immediately. ¹²So he said, "A nobleman went off to a distant country to obtain the kingship for himself and then to return. ¹³He called ten of his servants and gave them ten gold coins and told them, 'Engage in trade with these until I return.' ¹⁴His fellow citizens, however, despised him and sent a delegation after him to announce, 'We do not want this man to be our king.' ¹⁵But when he returned after obtaining the kingship, he had the servants called, to whom he had given the money, to learn what they had gained by trading. ¹⁶The first came forward and said, 'Sir, your gold coin has earned ten additional ones.' ¹⁷He replied, 'Well done, good servant! You have been faithful in this very small matter; take charge of ten cities.' ¹⁸Then the second came and reported, 'Your gold coin, sir, has earned five more.' ¹⁹And to this servant too he said, 'You, take charge of five cities.' ²⁰Then the

continue

bidder. For his part, the tax collector would then have to pay his contracted amount to the Romans as well as collect the fiscal revenues for them. Anything over and beyond those sums was his to keep. Failing to meet his payments would mean the Romans could confiscate his property and sell him and his family into slavery. Zacchaeus's position as the chief tax collector meant that lesser officials would have bidden for their offices from him, and if they did not produce the payment, Zacchaeus would have applied the appropriate penalties. In a word, Zacchaeus was very wealthy, and the resentment against him would have been very strong.

Despite his occupation, Zacchaeus is determined to see Jesus, even if it means looking foolish in doing so. Scholars are divided on whether to read the verbs "give" and "repay," which grammatically are in the present tense in Greek (v. 8), as present or future. In other words, is Zacchaeus boasting of present practices or making a statement of repentance to guide his future action? His hasty explanation to Jesus is heartfelt, for it would be of no advantage to him, an extortionist, to heed a wandering prophet or wonder-worker. Furthermore, the fact that he does show knowledge of wrongdoing manifests the salvation that is visiting him. If Jesus comes "to seek and to save what was lost" (v. 10), Zacchaeus must be a sinner. Zacchaeus the sinner can make a claim of being a descendant of Abraham, and his earnest desire to get a glimpse of Jesus is proof enough that that is what he desires.

19:11-27 The parable of the ten gold coins

Matthew and Luke differ in the telling of this parable, which, in large part, comes from Q overlapping slightly with Mark 13:34. A major difference between the two is that Luke also has a subtext discussing servants who do not want this particular nobleman to rule over them. This subtext may have as its origin Rome's choice of placing Archelaus, son of Herod the Great, on the throne at the death of his father. Because of his tyrannical and nearly sadistic behavior, the Jews petitioned Rome to have him removed. Rome responded by giving him only one-third of Herod's kingdom and eventually banishing him completely because of his excessive cruelty and incompetence.

Of lesser importance is Matthew's use of *talaton* (25:15) and Luke's *mna* as the denomination of the currency involved, which is translated here as "gold coins" (v. 13). A *mna* ("mina") would be worth about one hundred days' wages, and a *talanton* ("talent") sixty times as much.

Luke introduces the passage by noting that the traveling party was near Jerusalem and that some were supposing that the kingdom of God was about to appear. The parable addresses some of these points. The absentee nobleman returns without notice and thus surprises his servants. The first two servants are prepared for his sudden reappearance and are able to produce interest on the money given them; the third is not so concerned and has only a handkerchief with the original amount. It should be emphasized that the servants are commanded to use the money in such a manner as to earn more; thus the third servant was not only foolish but also disobedient.

As a story that follows the passage about the rich Zacchaeus, this parable gives an example on the proper way to use riches. The metaphor demonstrates that goods are to be employed for the upbuilding of the kingdom, and goods that are not used for this purpose will be taken away, as we see done with the third servant's *mna*.

The Lukan subtext plays a role in this passage by representing absolute refusal on the part of some to acknowledge the kingdom of God at all, whether in Jesus' first coming or in his second. Luke concludes this subtext within the same passage by having the nobleman slay the opposition. Many often cite this passage as an example of Lukan anti-Semitism. There is nothing in it, however, to suggest that those who receive the nobleman/Christ are Gentiles or that those who do not are Jews.

With this parable Jesus' journey to Jerusalem, which begins at 9:51, has reached its destination.

other servant came and said, 'Sir, here is your gold coin; I kept it stored away in a handkerchief, ²¹for I was afraid of you, because you are a demanding person; you take up what you did not lay down and you harvest what you did not plant.' ²²He said to him, 'With your own words I shall condemn you, you wicked servant. You knew I was a demanding person, taking up what I did not lay down and harvesting what I did not plant; ²³why did you not put my money in a bank? Then on my return I would have collected it with interest.' ²⁴And to those standing by he said, 'Take the gold coin from him and give it to the servant who has ten.' ²⁵But they said to him, 'Sir, he has ten gold coins.' ²⁶'I tell you, to everyone who has, more will be given, but from the one who has not, even what he has will be taken away. ²⁷Now as for those enemies of mine who did not want me as their king, bring them here and slay them before me.'"

VI: The Teaching Ministry in Jerusalem

The Entry into Jerusalem

²⁸After he had said this, he proceeded on his journey up to Jerusalem. ²⁹As he drew near to

continue

THE TEACHING MINISTRY IN JERUSALEM

Luke 19:28–21:38

Jesus has taught in Galilee, along the road to Judea, and now he will teach in the holy city. He arrives in Jerusalem, the city where he will meet his passion, death, and resurrection. With this background, his teaching takes on urgency.

19:28-40 The entry into Jerusalem

All four Gospels contain the account of Jesus' triumphal entry into Jerusalem. The respective narratives share a great deal of information, and any differences among them are seen in some minor details.

Bethphage and Bethany at the place called the Mount of Olives, he sent two of his disciples. ³⁰He said, "Go into the village opposite you, and as you enter it you will find a colt tethered on which no one has ever sat. Untie it and bring it here. ³¹And if anyone should ask you, 'Why are you untying it?' you will answer, 'The Master has need of it.'" ³²So those who had been sent went off and found everything just as he had told them. ³³And as they were untying the colt, its owners said to them, "Why are you untying this colt?" ³⁴They answered, "The Master has need of it." ³⁵So they brought it to Jesus, threw their cloaks over the colt, and helped Jesus to mount. ³⁶As he rode along, the people were spreading their cloaks on the road; ³⁷and now as he was approaching the slope of the Mount of Olives, the whole multitude of his disciples began to praise God aloud with joy for all the mighty deeds they had seen. ³⁸They proclaimed:

"Blessed is the king who comes in the name of the Lord.
Peace in heaven and glory in the highest."

³⁹Some of the Pharisees in the crowd said to him, "Teacher, rebuke your disciples." ⁴⁰He said in reply, "I tell you, if they keep silent, the stones will cry out!"

continue

For all three Synoptic writers, this triumphal entry is Jesus' first and only trip to Jerusalem, but John's Gospel, along with some details among the Synoptics, shows evidence that he may have gone to Jerusalem several times during his earthly ministry. The possibility of other sojourns to Jerusalem notwithstanding, what distinguishes this visit from all the others is the reception Jesus receives.

Bethphage and Bethany are both on the Roman road from Jericho to Jerusalem. We know from John 11:17-18 that Jesus has friends at the latter. This detail would explain how he could have made arrangements for the colt beforehand (Luke 19:29-31). All four Gospels show a heavy reliance on the prophecy in Zechariah 9:9 in their depictions of the scene.

In his descent from the Mount of Olives, Jesus encounters a rejoicing crowd. Matthew and Mark mention that the crowd also set garments and branches on the way; John specifies "palm branches" (12:13) but says nothing of garments, while Luke reads "cloaks" but does not include branches (v. 36). That three of the evangelists specify branches is used as evidence by some that the scene of the entry into Jerusalem described here actually refers to an earlier one at the time of the feast of Booths, or Sukkoth, a pilgrimage celebration falling in mid-September. Either Luke's source did not include branches, or Luke saw the reference as a superfluous detail. Whether or not the entry arises from the community's memory of a fall celebration at Sukkoth or a spring feast at Passover, the pertinent detail is that Jesus arrives in Jerusalem with throngs welcoming him.

The other evangelists have the crowd shouting "Hosanna," an Aramaic expression meaning "Save! I pray," a phrase unfamiliar to Luke's Gentile audience. Whereas the other Gospels have "*Blessed is he* who comes in the name of the Lord," Luke reads "*Blessed is the king*" (19:38, emphasis added). Luke's phrasing links Jesus' arrival in Jerusalem to the instruction on the imminent manifestation of the kingdom of God (see 13:35; 16:16; 18:15-17).

As an echo of the angels' hymn at the birth of Jesus (Luke 2:14), the crowd shouts out, "Peace in heaven and glory in the highest" (v. 38). What angels sang at Jesus' birth people now acclaim at his arrival.

Luke's depiction of the Pharisees in the crowd is less harsh than that of Matthew, who locates them in the temple after Jesus has cleansed it (Matt 21:16). Luke situates the Pharisees along the road leading into Jerusalem, and they seem more alarmed than hostile (19:39). Jesus' answer, a hyperbolic statement of fact, also serves as a challenge (19:40).

19:41-44 The lament over Jerusalem

The first lament over the city occurs in Luke 13:34-35 and is a Q saying (see Matt 23:37-39). Here, however, the reading appears only in Luke; both in theme and in imagery it is connected to the third and final reference to Jerusalem's destruction in Luke 21:21-24. Moreover, references to the siege (v. 43) are found in Jeremiah 6:6 and Ezekiel 4:2.

From the slopes of the Mount of Olives, Jesus would have seen the whole city spread out before him on the next hill. The temple with the doors to the holy of holies would have faced him. Tradition commemorates this scene at the Church of Dominus Flevit on the Mount of Olives. Archaeological evidence indicates that the most probable gate of Jesus' entry into the city rests underneath today's Golden Gate, which has been blocked since the eighth century. Today the Palm Sunday procession enters through St. Stephen's Gate, to the north of the Golden Gate along the eastern wall of the city.

19:45-48 The cleansing of the temple

Unlike Matthew or Mark, Luke concludes the entry into Jerusalem with the cleansing of the temple. Luke offers the most economic description of the event by not specifying the money changers, the animals, or even the "whip out of cords" (John 2:15). The phrase "My house shall be a house of prayer, but you have made it a den of thieves" is a blending of Isaiah 56:7 and Jeremiah 7:11.

The business transactions would have taken place in the Court of the Gentiles, surrounded by the Royal Portico, which was constructed for this very purpose. The merchants are not out of place in conducting their affairs in this area. In fact, the temple court served as the ground where worshipers proceeded from secular to sacred space by changing their pagan money to Jewish coins and purchasing ritually

The Lament for Jerusalem

[41]As he drew near, he saw the city and wept over it, [42]saying, "If this day you only knew what makes for peace—but now it is hidden from your eyes. [43]For the days are coming upon you when your enemies will raise a palisade against you; they will encircle you and hem you in on all sides. [44]They will smash you to the ground and your children within you, and they will not leave one stone upon another within you because you did not recognize the time of your visitation."

The Cleansing of the Temple

[45]Then Jesus entered the temple area and proceeded to drive out those who were selling things, [46]saying to them, "It is written, 'My house shall be a house of prayer, but you have made it a den of thieves.'" [47]And every day he was teaching in the temple area. The chief priests, the scribes, and the leaders of the people, meanwhile, were seeking to put him to death, [48]but they could find no way to accomplish their purpose because all the people were hanging on his words.

pure sacrificial victims. Jesus' anger, therefore, is not so much directed at those who have profaned a sacred zone with their mercantile greed; rather, he seems to be upset that any business should be associated with the temple at all. With incense, animals, oil, grain, and everything else needed for the sacrifices, the temple was a source of great income to the priests who had shares in most of the shops.

The glorious entry into Jerusalem ends on an ominous tone as the "chief priests, the scribes, and the leaders of the people" (v. 47), but not the Pharisees (19:39), plot to put Jesus to death.

EXPLORING LESSON THREE

1. If we are not to expect praise from God for doing our duty, how are we to gain salvation (17:7-10)? (See Rom 5:1-2; Eph 2:8.)

_____

_____

_____

_____

2. Ten lepers were cured, but the lone Samaritan leper has received more than a cure (17:7-10). What has he acquired and how did he acquire it?

_____

_____

_____

_____

3. What signs have you seen that might help us to know that the kingdom is among us?

_____

_____

_____

_____

4. Why was the Pharisee's careful fulfillment of his religious duties not acceptable to God? Why was the sinful tax collector justified before God (18:9-14)?

_____

_____

_____

_____

5. What do you think there is about children that make them models for adults in accepting the kingdom of God (18:15-17)?

_____

_____

_____

_____

6. What does the blind beggar outside Jericho "see" even before he is healed that many who are sighted cannot (18:35-43)?

_____

_____

_____

_____

7. a) Why were the crowds upset by Jesus' response to Zacchaeus (19:1-10)?

_____

_____

_____

  b) Why wouldn't Jesus require Zacchaeus to make the same total financial sacrifice he asked of the rich official in Luke 18:18-23?

_____

_____

_____

8. Where do you see Christians most effectively putting their earthly goods and resources to furthering the purposes of God's kingdom (19:11-26)? How have you shared in these efforts?

_____

_____

_____

9. Despite the joy with which many in Jerusalem greet Jesus as he enters the city, it is not long before Jesus is weeping over the city (19:28-40). What is the cause for his lament?

_____

_____

_____

10. Why do many of the religious leaders plot to put Jesus to death (19:45-48)? What is frustrating their efforts (19:48)?

_____

_____

_____

_____

CLOSING PRAYER

Prayer

"If this day you only knew what makes for peace . . ." (Luke 19:42)

Christ, bringer of wholeness (shalom), make us ambassadors for peace . . . in our inner selves, in our homes and workplaces, in our nation and world. May we recognize your presence, live by your precepts, and share from our abundance. We pray for situations in dire need of your peace, especially . . .

LESSON FOUR

Luke 20–22

Begin your personal study and group discussion with a simple and sincere prayer such as:

Prayer

> *God of all goodness, open my heart to hear you speak through the Gospel of Luke. Help me to journey faithfully toward Jerusalem with Jesus.*

Read the Bible text of Luke 20–22 found in the outside columns of pages 58–69, highlighting what stands out to you.

Read the accompanying commentary to add to your understanding.

Respond to the questions on pages 70–71, Exploring Lesson Four.

The closing prayer on page 72 is for your personal use and may be used at the end of group discussion.

CHAPTER 20

The Authority of Jesus Questioned

[1]One day as he was teaching the people in the temple area and proclaiming the good news, the chief priests and scribes, together with the elders, approached him [2]and said to him, "Tell us, by what authority are you doing these things? Or who is the one who gave you this authority?" [3]He said to them in reply, "I shall ask you a question. Tell me, [4]was John's baptism of heavenly or of human origin?" [5]They discussed this among themselves, and said, "If we say, 'Of heavenly origin,' he will say, 'Why did you not believe him?' [6]But if we say, 'Of human origin,' then all the people will stone us, for they are convinced that John was a prophet." [7]So they answered that they did not know from where it came. [8]Then Jesus said to them, "Neither shall I tell you by what authority I do these things."

The Parable of the Tenant Farmers

[9]Then he proceeded to tell the people this parable. "[A] man planted a vineyard, leased it to tenant farmers, and then went on a journey for a

continue

20:1-8 Questioning Jesus' authority

It is natural that after such a dramatic action as cleansing the temple, the priests, scribes, and elders would question Jesus' authority. All three Synoptic Gospels feature this account within the same narrative sequence. The authority of Jesus' teaching was a major question throughout his ministry, as the earlier Beelzebul controversy substantiates (Luke 11:14-23).

The temple leaders named here comprise the Sanhedrin, the highest Jewish council. It was composed of three groups: the priests (the high priest as well as the former high priests and family representatives); the scribes (legal scholars); and the elders (the chief members of the leading families and clans). Totaling seventy-one members, this group was the official Jewish court. In Jesus' time it had jurisdiction in religious and secular affairs only in Judea, but capital cases had to be recommended to the Roman governor for approval. It met in Jerusalem within the temple complex.

Jesus' reply is structured to avoid falling into the trap the officials have fashioned. If he were to say that his authority comes from the Lord God, as indeed it does, they could accuse him of blasphemy. As it is, Jesus' response insinuates such a conclusion without providing any incriminating evidence. By referring to John the Baptist, Jesus also draws from the prophetic tradition to make his defense. The comments of the temple leaders indicate the great regard for the Baptist that many of the people held. This devotion to John has implications for the development of Christianity.

20:9-19 The wicked tenant farmers

This parable strikes a note of recognition with both the people (v. 16) and the scribes and chief priests (v. 19). The whole piece is an analogy of the prophetic tradition. The one who plants the vineyard represents God; the tenant farmers, the people; the series of servants, the various prophets; the son, Jesus. The vineyard, as a fundamental symbol of Israel, and indeed the parable itself echo Isaiah (5:1-7), but it also surfaces as such in Psalm 80. Matthew (21:39) and Luke (20:15) reflect a literal understanding of the analogy by having the tenants cast the son from the vineyard before killing him (see Mark 12:8). Many think that a redactor tried to align the story with Jesus' crucifixion outside the walls of Jerusalem.

The context of this passage is, of course, the altercation Jesus has with the Sanhedrin in Luke 20:1-8. They refuse to recognize the hand of God in John the Baptist, whom Herod had put to death, and they continue in their refusal to see the hand of God in Jesus. Jesus ties his claim to divine authority by quoting from Psalm 118:22-23 (Luke 20:17), a verse that also resonates with Isaiah 8:14-15.

The schism motif enters here once again (see Luke 2:34). The leaders reject Jesus, but the people do not. God's promise takes root in the vineyard Israel, represented by the people's response, but this vineyard will also be shared with the Gentiles (v. 16).

Luke uses the parable's imagery and interpretation in Acts (18:6; 28:28). It also resurfaces in other New Testament writings, such as Romans 11:17-18 and 1 Peter 2:6-7.

20:20-26 Paying taxes to Caesar

The scribes and the chief priests are relentless in their attempts to trap Jesus by catching him off guard. After being shamed by the parable of the tenant farmers (20:9-19), they now send spies or agents to Jesus with hopes that he might incriminate himself by speaking against the empire. Jesus, however, sees through the ruse (20:23).

Roman coinage was highly symbolic for Jews concerned about paying taxes to the emperor. Engraved on the face of the denarius was the image of Tiberius Caesar—at the very least an offense against Jewish sensibilities, since it would go against the prohibition of graven idols. As a subject people, the Jews were required to use this currency for paying taxes and tribute to their occupiers. The question about the legality of paying taxes, therefore, involves the legality of handling idols to do so; the religious Jew should not be in contact with such pagan objects. Combined with these religious principles was the humiliation of paying the conqueror in the coin that transgressed their law code, thus forcing the Jews to participate in Roman paganism. Jesus' response not

long time. [10]At harvest time he sent a servant to the tenant farmers to receive some of the produce of the vineyard. But they beat the servant and sent him away empty-handed. [11]So he proceeded to send another servant, but him also they beat and insulted and sent away empty-handed. [12]Then he proceeded to send a third, but this one too they wounded and threw out. [13]The owner of the vineyard said, 'What shall I do? I shall send my beloved son; maybe they will respect him.' [14]But when the tenant farmers saw him they said to one another, 'This is the heir. Let us kill him that the inheritance may become ours.' [15]So they threw him out of the vineyard and killed him. What will the owner of the vineyard do to them? [16]He will come and put those tenant farmers to death and turn over the vineyard to others." When the people heard this, they exclaimed, "Let it not be so!" [17]But he looked at them and asked, "What then does this scripture passage mean:

'The stone which the builders rejected
has become the cornerstone'?

[18]Everyone who falls on that stone will be dashed to pieces; and it will crush anyone on whom it falls." [19]The scribes and chief priests sought to lay their hands on him at that very hour, but they feared the people, for they knew that he had addressed this parable to them.

Paying Taxes to the Emperor

[20]They watched him closely and sent agents pretending to be righteous who were to trap him in speech, in order to hand him over to the authority and power of the governor. [21]They posed this question to him, "Teacher, we know that what you say and teach is correct, and you show no partiality, but teach the way of God in accordance with the truth. [22]Is it lawful for us to pay tribute to Caesar or not?" [23]Recognizing their craftiness he said to them, [24]"Show me a denarius; whose image and name does it bear?" They replied, "Caesar's." [25]So he said to them, "Then repay to Caesar what belongs to Caesar and to God what

continue

belongs to God." [26]They were unable to trap him by something he might say before the people, and so amazed were they at his reply that they fell silent.

The Question about the Resurrection

[27]Some Sadducees, those who deny that there is a resurrection, came forward and put this question to him, [28]saying, "Teacher, Moses wrote for us, 'If someone's brother dies leaving a wife but no child, his brother must take the wife and raise up descendants for his brother.' [29]Now there were seven brothers; the first married a woman but died childless. [30]Then the second [31]and the third married her, and likewise all the seven died childless. [32]Finally the woman also died. [33]Now at the resurrection whose wife will that woman be? For all seven had been married to her." [34]Jesus said to them, "The children of this age marry and are given in marriage; [35]but those who are deemed worthy to attain to the coming age and to the resurrection of the dead neither marry nor are given in marriage. [36]They can no longer die, for they are like angels; and they are the children of God because they are the ones who will rise. [37]That the dead will rise even Moses made known in the passage about the bush, when he called 'Lord' the God of Abraham, the God of Isaac, and the God of Jacob; [38]and he is not God of the dead, but of the living, for to him all are alive." [39]Some of the scribes said in reply, "Teacher, you have answered well." [40]And they no longer dared to ask him anything.

continue

only avoids the trap the leaders set for him but also calls into question the meaning of true, righteous behavior.

Jesus gains the upper hand against his adversaries by not pitting allegiance to Rome against fidelity to the Torah (the holy writings of the Jewish religion, especially the first five books of the Old Testament). The lesson is that one is not defiled by paying taxes to Rome.

Being righteous before God is an issue deeper than paying taxes to a pagan power.

The idea of rendering to Caesar the things that are Caesar's and to God the things that are God's has often been mistakenly used as an injunction for keeping religious and ethical questions separate from political or secular policies. Correctly read through an eschatological lens, Jesus' aphorism states that the things of this world have an impact on the next, while standards of the age to come should have an influence on this present life.

20:27-40 Sadducees and the resurrection

The Sadducees, opponents of the Pharisees, particularly over the teachings on the resurrection, are the next group to question Jesus with an eye toward tripping him up. Not much is known about them except that they were aristocratic conservatives tied to the temple cult (unlike the Pharisees, who promoted the synagogue movement). The circumstance they describe is based on levirate marriage (Deut 25:5-6), whereby a widow's brother-in-law marries her to ensure that the lands stay in the first husband's family and that his name is carried on. Jesus responds by discussing first the nature of a resurrected life and then the basis of the resurrection in the Jewish tradition.

The resurrected life goes beyond the dimensions of earthly existence. Thus expectations and practices in this world do not hold in the next. Moreover, the resurrected life transcends this one (vv. 35, 36, 38). By citing Moses, Jesus taps the source of Jewish faith as well as the sole component of the Sadducees' teaching, for their belief extended no further than the first five books of Moses, often called the Torah or the Pentateuch.

Jesus' argument is impeccable. The scribes, who along with the Pharisees believe in the resurrection, affirm Jesus' answer; the Sadducees who brought up the matter, on the other hand, are silent (vv. 39-40).

Unlike the parallel accounts in Matthew 22:23-33 or Mark 12:18-27, Luke's version contains a teaching that supports celibate life (v. 35; see also Matt 19:12).

20:41-44 David's Son

Jesus' opponents would want to make sure that there is nothing about him which would suggest that he is the Messiah. At the same time, they have to acknowledge that the people see him as a great man, and therefore he could quite possibly be the one long promised by the prophets. At that time the tradition existed of a Messiah arising from David's line, a belief to which the infancy narratives attest. The narrative here draws on this tradition.

In verse 42 Jesus cites Psalm 110:1, a coronation psalm, which in the Greek Septuagint is reflected in this translation. In Psalm 110 the psalmist is speaking, and "Lord" (uppercase here) refers to Yahweh. The "lord" (lowercase here) is the king whom Yahweh is placing on the throne. In its New Testament interpretation, "Lord" still refers to Yahweh, but David the king is speaking. Consequently, "lord" represents a messianic figure who is greater than David. In these verses Jesus states that the term "lord" refers to himself.

The early church drew on this tradition of a Davidic Messiah both here and elsewhere, and this psalm was used as one of the Old Testament writings prefiguring Christ. The other Synoptics contain passages parallel to this one.

20:45-47 Denunciation of the scribes

Jesus, after defending himself before both the Pharisees and Sadducees, takes the offensive. Scribes, as ones who could read, write, and interpret texts, are synonymous with the Pharisees. As a scholarly religious class who knew the Torah and the oral tradition with all the astuteness of master lawyers, they expected honor and deference as their due. As with all professions, there were good and bad members among them. Even Jesus was considered by his disciples to be a teacher.

The condemnation Jesus levels here (vv. 46-47) is directed toward those who are a part of the temple power structure and use their status and expertise for personal advantage at the expense of the poor and unprivileged. This short passage also reflects the debates between church and synagogue in the early days of the

The Question about David's Son

⁴¹Then he said to them, "How do they claim that the Messiah is the Son of David? ⁴²For David himself in the Book of Psalms says:

'The Lord said to my lord,
"Sit at my right hand
⁴³till I make your enemies your footstool." '

⁴⁴Now if David calls him 'lord,' how can he be his son?"

Denunciation of the Scribes

⁴⁵Then, within the hearing of all the people, he said to [his] disciples, ⁴⁶"Be on guard against the scribes, who like to go around in long robes and love greetings in marketplaces, seats of honor in synagogues, and places of honor at banquets. ⁴⁷They devour the houses of widows and, as a pretext, recite lengthy prayers. They will receive a very severe condemnation."

CHAPTER 21

The Poor Widow's Contribution

¹When he looked up he saw some wealthy people putting their offerings into the treasury ²and he noticed a poor widow putting in two small coins. ³He said, "I tell you truly, this poor widow put in more than all the rest; ⁴for those others have all made offerings from their surplus

continue

Christian movement. It sets the context for what follows in Luke 21:1-4.

21:1-4 The poor widow's contribution

Luke shares this story with Mark (see Mark 12:41-44). Each coin is a lepton, which is worth slightly more than one-hundredth of a denarius. Since a denarius is a day's wage, the widow places about one-fiftieth of a day's living into the treasury, and, as Jesus remarks, this is her whole livelihood.

wealth, but she, from her poverty, has offered her whole livelihood."

The Destruction of the Temple Foretold

⁵While some people were speaking about how the temple was adorned with costly stones and votive offerings, he said, ⁶"All that you see here— the days will come when there will not be left a stone upon another stone that will not be thrown down."

The Signs of the End

⁷Then they asked him, "Teacher, when will this happen? And what sign will there be when all these things are about to happen?" ⁸He answered, "See that you not be deceived, for many will come in my name, saying, 'I am he,' and 'The time has come.' Do not follow them! ⁹When you hear of wars and insurrections, do not be terrified; for such things must happen first, but it will not immediately be the end." ¹⁰Then he said to them, "Nation will rise against nation, and kingdom against kingdom. ¹¹There will be powerful earthquakes, famines, and plagues from place to place; and awesome sights and mighty signs will come from the sky.

continue

Many hold that this story shows the widow's pious devotion, and she has become a model of religious dedication in that all should give from their sustenance and not their superfluity. The context, however, suggests another interpretation.

Jesus' first order of business upon entering Jerusalem is to go to the temple and drive out those "selling things" (19:45). His violent response to revenues generated by temple worship in that section of the Lukan narrative would be indicative of anger here. In addition, in the preceding passage Jesus has denounced the scribes for "devour[ing] the houses of widows" (Luke 20:47). Jesus is upset at seeing a poor woman think that God's will demanded

making herself destitute so that others could become rich.

21:5-6 The destruction of the temple foretold

All three Synoptics contain the prediction of the temple's destruction. The building of Herod's temple, the edifice under discussion in this passage, began in 19 B.C. and was still under construction during Jesus' lifetime (see John 2:20). The whole complex was completed in A.D. 64, only to be totally razed six years later during the First Jewish Revolt. When it was completed, it was considered one of the most beautiful buildings in the whole Roman Empire. The people's awe and wonder at the stones were totally justified. As the house of God, its destruction would seem like the end of the world in the minds of the people (see Josephus, *Ant.* 15.11.1-7 and *J.W.* 4-5).

Is the prediction of the destruction a *vaticinium ex eventu*, that is, a foretelling after the event? If so, then the writer, Luke, is theologizing about the temple's destruction by placing a prediction of it on the lips of Jesus. On the other hand, anyone sensitive to the political climate of the day would know that the tensions would someday explode, resulting in catastrophic disaster for the nation.

This account forms a bridge between the story of the poor widow (21:1-4) and Luke's apocalyptic section (21:7-36).

21:7-11 The signs of the end

Luke 21:7-36 forms the Lukan apocalypse, but it is not the only place in the third Gospel where apocalyptic imagery occurs (see Luke 17:22-37). Matthew 24 and Mark 13 have parallel passages.

The great part of the language and metaphor used here is characteristic of apocalyptic writing: signs, natural upheavals, disasters, wars, persecution, and a call to vigilance. Apocalyptic language is often, but not exclusively, associated with eschatological teaching, and in this sense this section is more rightly called the Lukan eschatological discourse. By definition, *eschatology* deals with the interpretation of the end times, the fulfillment of history, and culmination of human destiny. In general, we can say that this section shows eschatological concerns in apocalyptic language.

Rarely has anyone been able to identify conclusively the particular historical references to the events mentioned in verses 7-11. There has never been a time in human history when wars, earthquakes, famines, and plagues have not been a part of the picture. Since any one of these events and phenomena can occur without warning or notice, it is better to be prepared, and preparation consists in always looking for Christ in every person and circumstance.

21:12-19 The coming persecution

The early Christian community faced persecution from the home as well as from rulers of both synagogue and state. These Gospel verses, in non-apocalyptic vocabulary, are meant to console and strengthen the believers facing their tribulation.

Verses 14-15 form a doublet with Luke 12:11-12.

21:20-24 The great tribulation

The words that Jesus speaks in this passage ring true to the history of the destruction of Jerusalem.

The Roman general Titus arrived at Jerusalem and set up his main camp about one mile north of the Mount of Olives at Mount Scopus in the spring of A.D. 70. By July his men set to constructing a siege wall around the city to prevent the people of Jerusalem from escaping while protecting the Roman soldiers from Jewish raiding parties. Since such procedures were standard Roman military operations, the description in these verses need not be considered peculiar to the Roman siege in A.D. 70. Nonetheless, the arrival of the Romans came with unexpected suddenness, and internecine fighting among various Jewish sects had reduced the food stores, so that starvation became a major problem within the city (see Josephus, J.W. 5.2-3i). On August 28 (Ninth of Ab, by coincidence the same day the Babylo-

The Coming Persecution

[12]"Before all this happens, however, they will seize and persecute you, they will hand you over to the synagogues and to prisons, and they will have you led before kings and governors because of my name. [13]It will lead to your giving testimony. [14]Remember, you are not to prepare your defense beforehand, [15]for I myself shall give you a wisdom in speaking that all your adversaries will be powerless to resist or refute. [16]You will even be handed over by parents, brothers, relatives, and friends, and they will put some of you to death. [17]You will be hated by all because of my name, [18]but not a hair on your head will be destroyed. [19]By your perseverance you will secure your lives.

The Great Tribulation

[20]"When you see Jerusalem surrounded by armies, know that its desolation is at hand. [21]Then those in Judea must flee to the mountains. Let those within the city escape from it, and let those in the countryside not enter the city, [22]for these days are the time of punishment when all the scriptures are fulfilled. [23]Woe to pregnant women and nursing mothers in those days, for a terrible calamity will come upon the earth and a wrathful judgment upon this people. [24]They will fall by the edge of the sword and be taken as captives to all the Gentiles; and Jerusalem will be trampled

continue

nians breached the city some six hundred years earlier), Jerusalem fell to the Romans. Any Jewish survivors were taken captive, and the city, including the temple, was razed to the ground.

Old Testament prophecies are employed in the description: Hosea 9:7 in Luke 21:22; Sirach 28:18; Deuteronomy 28:64; and Zechariah 12:3 in Luke 21:24. Tradition has it that the Christians in the city fled to the city of Pella in present-day Jordan at the outbreak of hostilities. The "time of the Gentiles" (v. 24) foreshadows the great missionary ventures outlined in the Acts of the Apostles.

underfoot by the Gentiles until the times of the Gentiles are fulfilled.

The Coming of the Son of Man

[25]"There will be signs in the sun, the moon, and the stars, and on earth nations will be in dismay, perplexed by the roaring of the sea and the waves. [26]People will die of fright in anticipation of what is coming upon the world, for the powers of the heavens will be shaken. [27]And then they will see the Son of Man coming in a cloud with power and great glory. [28]But when these signs begin to happen, stand erect and raise your heads because your redemption is at hand."

The Lesson of the Fig Tree

[29]He taught them a lesson. "Consider the fig tree and all the other trees. [30]When their buds burst open, you see for yourselves and know that summer is now near; [31]in the same way, when you see these things happening, know that the kingdom of God is near. [32]Amen, I say to you, this generation will not pass away until all these things have taken place. [33]Heaven and earth will pass away, but my words will not pass away.

Exhortation to be Vigilant

[34]"Beware that your hearts do not become drowsy from carousing and drunkenness and the anxieties of daily life, and that day catch you by surprise [35]like a trap. For that day will assault everyone who lives on the face of the earth. [36]Be vigilant at all times and pray that you have the strength to escape the tribulations that are imminent and to stand before the Son of Man."

continue

21:25-28 The coming of the Son of Man

The scene shifts from Jerusalem to the whole world. The language returns to apocalyptic terminology, drawing on Isaiah, Joel, Zephaniah, and Daniel. What has happened to Jerusalem may be a harbinger of the Son of Man's visitation upon the earth, but it is not an immediate warning signal. The scene is not bleak, however. The astral signs and natural calamities serve to notify that redemption is at hand. Just as the people of Jerusalem were mixed in their reception of Jesus, so too will the world be at his second coming.

21:29-33 The lesson of the fig tree

If people can read the signs in nature, they should be willing and able to read the signs of their deliverance.

The reference to "this generation" (v. 32) is ambiguous. In one sense, there is every reason to believe that many in the then contemporary generation would not pass away until after the First Jewish Revolt. On the other hand, if "all these things" refers to upheavals in nature ushering in the Son of Man, "this generation" is a timeless reference to the world; the eschaton, or end time, is always imminent.

21:34-36 Exhortation to be vigilant

One must stand with apocalyptic vigilance. The note of surprise resurfaces here (v. 34). Under an imminent understanding of the eschaton, the coming of the Son of Man will always be sudden. The directive to pray (v. 36) is a particularly Lukan concern. Jesus prays in the Garden of Gethsemane (22:39-46), and his note of "tribulations" (v. 36) looks toward his own passion.

21:37-38 Conclusion to the ministry in Jerusalem

During the pilgrimage feasts most people, particularly those without relatives in Jerusalem proper, camped on the fields and hills surrounding the city. The Mount of Olives appears to have been one such place.

Despite the discourse on the temple and Jerusalem, Luke is ambiguous toward both. Jesus teaches in the temple even as he speaks against it. Furthermore, in the Acts of the Apostles the temple becomes the site of many events in the ministry of Peter, Paul, and the other disciples. Jesus' public ministry ends with these verses.

THE PASSION

Luke 22:1–23:56

The passion narrative, the nucleus of the kerygma, forms the oldest part of the Gospel tradition. The accounts of the four evangelists show the greatest similarity with each other in this section. Nonetheless, each evangelist shapes the information to fit the theological architecture of his respective Gospel. In Luke, the themes found all along reach their climax. The schism motif, the great reversal, and the victory over evil all manifest Jesus' reclamation of the cosmos from Satan's clutches as Christ brings the promise of future glory to all.

22:1-6 The conspiracy against Jesus

The diabolical force that has been mounting challenge against Jesus from the very beginning (Luke 4:1-13) increases in intensity here when Satan "enter[s] into Judas" (v. 3). In Luke's narrative, now is the "time" (4:13) for which the devil has been waiting.

Both priests and scribes are at the center of the conspiracy, but by making Judas his agent, Satan fashions a more serious inroad against Jesus. Hence the passion is not merely a human drama; rather, it is an event that involves the whole cosmos. Luke's account of Jesus' passion, with its collusion between Satan and Judas, departs from the synoptic presentation and aligns itself more closely with the Johannine text, and in so doing respects the cosmological nature of the drama.

One of the major pilgrimage feasts that brought thousands to Jerusalem, the feast of Unleavened Bread was originally an agrarian festival celebrated in the spring during the grain harvest. Passover began as a nomadic feast, also held in the spring, when people took their flocks of sheep and goats from the winter to summer feeding grounds. The Jewish practice at the time of Jesus had joined these two feasts into one commemorating the Exodus from Egypt.

For the Romans, this annual spring holiday posed a major security risk. The throngs of people, coupled with the nationalistic over-

---

Ministry in Jerusalem

[37]During the day, Jesus was teaching in the temple area, but at night he would leave and stay at the place called the Mount of Olives. [38]And all the people would get up early each morning to listen to him in the temple area.

VII: The Passion Narrative

CHAPTER 22

The Conspiracy against Jesus

[1]Now the feast of Unleavened Bread, called the Passover, was drawing near, [2]and the chief priests and the scribes were seeking a way to put him to death, for they were afraid of the people. [3]Then Satan entered into Judas, the one surnamed Iscariot, who was counted among the Twelve, [4]and he went to the chief priests and temple guards to discuss a plan for handing him over to them. [5]They were pleased and agreed to pay him money. [6]He accepted their offer and sought a favorable opportunity to hand him over to them in the absence of a crowd.

Preparations for the Passover

[7]When the day of the Feast of Unleavened Bread arrived, the day for sacrificing the Passover

continue

---

tones inherent in the Exodus event, set the stage for riots and insurrection. The temple leaders, functioning as colonial lackeys of Rome, were well aware that Jesus was a popular figure who fulfilled the messianic expectations of a great many. A conspiracy between Judas, the chief priests, and the guards that tries to find an opportunity to arrest Jesus away from the crowd is indicative of the volatility of the situation (v. 6).

22:7-38 The Passover meal

According to the synoptic dating, the meal takes place on Passover (v. 7); in John's Gospel (13:1) it is on the day before. Jesus must have lamb, [8]he sent out Peter and John, instructing them, "Go and make preparations for us to eat the Passover." [9]They asked him, "Where do you want us to make the preparations?" [10]And he answered them, "When you go into the city, a man will meet you carrying a jar of water. Follow him into the house that he enters [11]and say to the master of the house, 'The teacher says to you, "Where is the guest room where I may eat the Passover with my disciples?" ' [12]He will show you a large upper room that is furnished. Make the preparations there." [13]Then they went off and found everything exactly as he had told them, and there they prepared the Passover.

The Last Supper

[14]When the hour came, he took his place at table with the apostles. [15]He said to them, "I have eagerly desired to eat this Passover with you before I suffer, [16]for, I tell you, I shall not eat it [again] until there is fulfillment in the kingdom of God." [17]Then he took a cup, gave thanks, and said, "Take this and share it among yourselves; [18]for I tell you [that] from this time on I shall not drink of the fruit of the vine until the kingdom of God comes." [19]Then he took the bread, said the blessing, broke it, and gave it to them, saying, "This is my body, which will be given for you; do this in memory of me." [20]And likewise the cup after they had eaten, saying, "This cup is the new covenant in my blood, which will be shed for you.

The Betrayal Foretold

[21]"And yet behold, the hand of the one who is to betray me is with me on the table; [22]for the Son of Man indeed goes as it has been determined; but woe to that man by whom he is betrayed." [23]And they began to debate among themselves who among them would do such a deed.

The Role of the Disciples

[24]Then an argument broke out among them about which of them should be regarded as the greatest. [25]He said to them, "The kings of the

continue

had disciples and acquaintances in Jerusalem for him to give such specific instructions to Peter and John (vv. 10-12). For this reason, many scholars believe that Jesus went to Jerusalem on several occasions and not just this once, as Luke and the other Synoptics portray. Since women alone generally carried water jars, a man walking with one would attract attention. Jesus leaves the exact location for the meal unspecified to maintain secrecy in the face of impending danger. The Greek for "guest room" (v. 11) is *kataluma* (see 2:7).

It is nearly impossible to determine with absolute accuracy the Jewish Seder, that is, the Passover meal, at this period of history. Nonetheless, all indications are that it involved a total of three blessings of the cup. Luke mentions two of them—one at the beginning of the meal and one at the end (vv. 17, 20). Paul's version of what has come to be called the "institution narrative" is remarkably similar to that of Luke here (see 1 Cor 11:23-26). The elements of the Exodus sacrifice, such as blood, are reinterpreted in the light of Christ's life. He sheds his blood to ensure the life of God's people (see Exod 12:12-16; 24:5-8).

The mention of the betrayer's hand (v. 21), whom the reader knows to be Judas Iscariot (22:3), sparks an argument at the table. Jesus intervenes with a lesson that continues the reversal theme introduced in the Magnificat (Luke 1:46-55). Here at the Last Supper, Jesus gives a more positive rendition of the theme: disciples should reverse the roles themselves in order to further the kingdom. Doing so leads to true greatness (22:24-30).

Just as Jesus predicts the role of Judas, though unnamed (vv. 21-23), so too does he predict Peter's denial (vv. 31-34). The devil has already claimed Judas, and now he is attempting to take the rest of the Twelve, Peter included, as Jesus is well aware. Jesus needs Peter to support the others (v. 32), but Peter will falter, as Jesus predicts. Luke alone acknowledges in this manner the cosmic battle Jesus' life and death entail.

In a crisis one should be sure to prepare for the worst, a worry not present in easier times

(vv. 35-37). The Twelve still have difficulty understanding Jesus' teaching and mission. They take his metaphors literally, and he loses patience (v. 38).

22:39-53 The agony and arrest

Jesus goes to the Mount of Olives, as is his custom (21:37-38). Prayer is a key element in the makeup of Luke's Gospel, and at this moment Jesus prays. The disciples, however, oblivious to the seriousness of events, fall asleep.

What is commonly called **"the agony in the garden"** is actually portrayed thus only in Luke's version. Luke calls the "garden" the Mount of Olives and uses the Greek word *agonia* ("anguish, intense struggle") to evoke the kind of preparation that athletes undergo before an athletic contest. Luke emphasizes the intensity by describing sweat "like drops of blood," but these lines (22:43-44) are missing from the oldest and best manuscripts. Nonetheless, Christian theology and art have interpreted Jesus' time of prayer on the Mount of Olives as an ultimate test of his willingness to accept his Father's will.

Many reliable ancient manuscripts do not include verses 43-44, but many other ones, just as reliable, do. Whether these verses belong in the Lukan text is a debated issue, but the balance tips for their inclusion. In Luke's temptation scene (4:1-13), the devil "depart[s] for a time," and because he does, Luke has no need of including the ministering angels found in Matthew 4:11 and Mark 1:13. In Luke's narrative, Satan's time comes at the passion (22:3, 31). With Luke, therefore, the angel comes to minister to Jesus during his agony, the time and place where Satan exhibits his fury; it is Satan's "hour, the time for the power of darkness" (v. 53), an "hour" that will last through the crucifixion (see 23:44).

Gentiles lord it over them and those in authority over them are addressed as 'Benefactors'; [26]but among you it shall not be so. Rather, let the greatest among you be as the youngest, and the leader as the servant. [27]For who is greater: the one seated at table or the one who serves? Is it not the one seated at table? I am among you as the one who serves. [28]It is you who have stood by me in my trials; [29]and I confer a kingdom on you, just as my Father has conferred one on me, [30]that you may eat and drink at my table in my kingdom; and you will sit on thrones judging the twelve tribes of Israel.

Peter's Denial Foretold

[31]"Simon, Simon, behold Satan has demanded to sift all of you like wheat, [32]but I have prayed that your own faith may not fail; and once you have turned back, you must strengthen your brothers." [33]He said to him, "Lord, I am prepared to go to prison and to die with you." [34]But he replied, "I tell you, Peter, before the cock crows this day, you will deny three times that you know me."

Instructions for the Time of Crisis

[35]He said to them, "When I sent you forth without a money bag or a sack or sandals, were you in need of anything?" "No, nothing," they replied. [36]He said to them, "But now one who has a money bag should take it, and likewise a sack, and one who does not have a sword should sell his cloak and buy one. [37]For I tell you that this scripture must be fulfilled in me, namely, 'He was counted among the wicked'; and indeed what is written about me is coming to fulfillment." [38]Then they said, "Lord, look, there are two swords here." But he replied, "It is enough!"

The Agony in the Garden

[39]Then going out he went, as was his custom, to the Mount of Olives, and the disciples followed him. [40]When he arrived at the place he said to them, "Pray that you may not undergo the test."

continue

[41]After withdrawing about a stone's throw from them and kneeling, he prayed, [42]saying, "Father, if you are willing, take this cup away from me; still, not my will but yours be done." [[43]And to strengthen him an angel from heaven appeared to him. [44]He was in such agony and he prayed so fervently that his sweat became like drops of blood falling on the ground.] [45]When he rose from prayer and returned to his disciples, he found them sleeping from grief. [46]He said to them, "Why are you sleeping? Get up and pray that you may not undergo the test."

The Betrayal and Arrest of Jesus

[47]While he was still speaking, a crowd approached and in front was one of the Twelve, a man named Judas. He went up to Jesus to kiss him. [48]Jesus said to him, "Judas, are you betraying the Son of Man with a kiss?" [49]His disciples realized what was about to happen, and they asked, "Lord, shall we strike with a sword?" [50]And one of them struck the high priest's servant and cut off his right ear. [51]But Jesus said in reply, "Stop, no more of this!" Then he touched the servant's ear and healed him. [52]And Jesus said to the chief priests and temple guards and elders who had come for him, "Have you come out as against a robber, with swords and clubs? [53]Day after day I was with you in the temple area, and you did not seize me; but this is your hour, the time for the power of darkness."

Peter's Denial of Jesus

[54]After arresting him they led him away and took him into the house of the high priest; Peter was following at a distance. [55]They lit a fire in the middle of the courtyard and sat around it, and Peter sat down with them. [56]When a maid saw him seated in the light, she looked intently at him and said, "This man too was with him." [57]But he denied it saying, "Woman, I do not know him." [58]A short while later someone else saw him and said, "You too are one of them"; but Peter answered, "My friend, I am not." [59]About an hour

continue

Jesus' emotional state is fragile, and he prays. The road from Jerusalem to the Judean desert passes up and over the Mount of Olives. He agonizes over a decision on whether to stay or to flee, and the tension brings him to the verge of a nervous breakdown (v. 44). A rare medical condition called "hematidrosis," a bloody sweat, sometimes occurs in people under extreme duress. For this reason some speculate that Jesus actually sweat blood. The text reads, however, that his "sweat became like drops of blood," that is, heavy and thick.

Judas finds his opportunity to hand Jesus over as he had planned with the temple authorities. It is unclear from Luke whether he actually kisses Jesus, although Matthew and Mark say so. Luke, the evangelist of "sweet mercy," is the only Synoptic to have Jesus heal the ear of the high priest's slave, while John's is the only Gospel to state the slave's name (John 18:10). Jesus' followers are ready to fight, but Jesus forbids them (v. 51).

22:54-65 Peter's denial

Peter's denial is recounted in all four Gospels.

Peter, always impetuous, follows as Jesus is led to the house of the high priest. Presumably the other disciples are hiding or at least keeping their distance from Jerusalemites. Fear overpowers Peter's usually forward manner, and he denies any contact or involvement with Jesus. Luke mentions that Jesus looks at Peter once the crowing has stopped. The glance acts as an acknowledgement of the action; Peter cannot hide from Jesus or himself, so he goes off weeping bitterly. His denial, followed by his remorse, displays Satan's near capture of him as well as the power of Jesus' prayer, for Peter, unlike Judas, will return (22:32).

Jesus spends the night in the house of the high priest, located, according to tradition and some scholars, on the southwestern slope of the city at a site currently called St. Peter in Gallicantu. Other archaeologists place the high priest's house on top of the western hill. Luke mentions only the priests and temple guards as ridiculing and demeaning Jesus here (vv. 64-65); the Romans will have their turn (23:36-37).

22:66-71 Jesus before the Sanhedrin

The Sanhedrin heard all cases dealing with Jewish law but could not inflict capital punishment, the penalty for blasphemy. Thus Jesus also has to undergo proceedings in a Roman court. The Sanhedrin uses this opportunity, therefore, to build their case before presenting him to Pilate, where they supplement the charge against Jesus with treasonable offenses (23:2).

The interrogation scene echoes details from the annunciation of Jesus' birth (1:32, 35). Jesus responds to the questions by quoting from Daniel 7:13, a text that asserts the divinity of the Messiah and thereby places the Sanhedrin under Jesus' judgment. They recognize his ploy immediately and hasten him to Pontius Pilate.

later, still another insisted, "Assuredly, this man too was with him, for he also is a Galilean." [60]But Peter said, "My friend, I do not know what you are talking about." Just as he was saying this, the cock crowed, [61]and the Lord turned and looked at Peter; and Peter remembered the word of the Lord, how he had said to him, "Before the cock crows today, you will deny me three times." [62]He went out and began to weep bitterly. [63]The men who held Jesus in custody were ridiculing and beating him. [64]They blindfolded him and questioned him, saying, "Prophesy! Who is it that struck you?" [65]And they reviled him in saying many other things against him.

Jesus before the Sanhedrin

[66]When day came the council of elders of the people met, both chief priests and scribes, and they brought him before their Sanhedrin. [67]They said, "If you are the Messiah, tell us," but he replied to them, "If I tell you, you will not believe, [68]and if I question, you will not respond. [69]But from this time on the Son of Man will be seated at the right hand of the power of God." [70]They all asked, "Are you then the Son of God?" He replied to them, "You say that I am." [71]Then they said, "What further need have we for testimony? We have heard it from his own mouth."

EXPLORING LESSON FOUR

1. Why wouldn't the religious leaders answer Jesus' question concerning the nature of John's baptism (20:1-8)? (See Matt 3:1-11.)

2. Why was the denarius, the coin used to pay tax to Rome, especially problematic for some scrupulous Jews in Jesus' time (20:20-26)?

3. What did Jesus say to the Sadducees concerning the evidence for the resurrection in the law of Moses (20:37-38)? (See Exod 3:6; Deut 5:26.)

4. What are two possible but quite different understandings of Jesus' response to the poor widow's contribution (21:1-4)? (See 20:46-47.)

5. Many of the signs concerning the end of time have been present throughout world history, but we must always be prepared for the second coming (21:7-11, 34-36). What can we do to stay prepared for Jesus' return?

6. a) What did Jesus identify with the bread and the second cup of the last meal he shared with his disciples (22:14-20)?

_____

_____

_____

   b) How has Jesus' gift of himself in this meal made a difference in your own life?

_____

_____

_____

7. What aspect of the Last Supper do only Luke and Paul share (22:17-20; 1 Cor 11:23-26)? How do their accounts provide an additional connection to the Passover meals of the time?

_____

_____

_____

8. How is Jesus' agony in the garden (22:39-46) linked to his temptation in the wilderness following his baptism (4:1-3)?

_____

_____

_____

9. What does Luke tell us triggered Peter's tears after denying Jesus (22:54-62)? Ignatian prayer teaches us to picture as vividly as possible a scene depicted in the Bible and, through our imagination, to place ourselves within it. Try doing that with this passage and then jot down any spiritual insights gained from praying this passage.

_____

_____

_____

_____

10. Why would Jesus' statements concerning the Son of Man and the Son of God be considered a threat to the authority of the Sanhedrin (22:66-71)? (See Dan 7:13-14.)

_____

_____

_____

CLOSING PRAYER

Prayer

"Let the greatest among you be as the youngest, and the leader as the servant."

(Luke 22:26)

Jesus, you teach us the way of reversal—the first shall be last and the leader shall be servant. You upset our usual ways of seeing the world so that we might recognize and imitate you. Help us also to embrace a way of life where service is a higher priority than status. We pray for the needs of our neighbors and our world, especially . . .

LESSON FIVE

Luke 23–24

Begin your personal study and group discussion with a simple and sincere prayer such as:

Prayer

God of all goodness, open my heart to hear you speak through the Gospel of Luke. Help me to journey faithfully toward Jerusalem with Jesus.

Read the Bible text of Luke 23–24 found in the outside columns of pages 74–82, highlighting what stands out to you.

Read the accompanying commentary to add to your understanding.

Respond to the questions on pages 83–84, Exploring Lesson Five.

The closing prayer on page 85 is for your personal use and may be used at the end of group discussion.

CHAPTER 23

Jesus before Pilate

¹Then the whole assembly of them arose and brought him before Pilate. ²They brought charges against him, saying, "We found this man misleading our people; he opposes the payment of taxes to Caesar and maintains that he is the Messiah, a king." ³Pilate asked him, "Are you the king of the Jews?" He said to him in reply, "You say so." ⁴Pilate then addressed the chief priests and the crowds, "I find this man not guilty." ⁵But they were adamant and said, "He is inciting the people with his teaching throughout all Judea, from Galilee where he began even to here."

Jesus before Herod

⁶On hearing this Pilate asked if the man was a Galilean; ⁷and upon learning that he was under Herod's jurisdiction, he sent him to Herod who was in Jerusalem at that time. ⁸Herod was very glad to see Jesus; he had been wanting to see him for a long time, for he had heard about him and had been hoping to see him perform some sign. ⁹He questioned him at length, but he gave him no answer. ¹⁰The chief priests and scribes, meanwhile, stood by accusing him harshly. ¹¹[Even] Herod and his soldiers treated him contemptuously and mocked him, and after clothing him in

continue

23:1-5 Jesus before Pilate

Like every colonial power in history, the Romans made friends with a certain class of the native population. This enabled them to impose foreign rule by wearing a domestic mask. In Palestine the temple priests were the class whom the Romans supported and who supported the Romans. They received revenues from performing the sacrifices of the people. In addition, they had shares in many of the shops and food providers of Jerusalem, and during the great pilgrimage feasts like Passover, this provided them with a healthy income. Roman stability secured the priests' status.

The Romans, on the other hand, needed the priests to guarantee their legitimacy. The priests enabled the Romans to appear as supporters of the Jewish faith. They acted as mediators between the emperor and the Jewish people, and as such they made Roman tax collection easier. In sum, there was an elite ruling class composed of Romans and Jews, both of whom had a vested interest in keeping the peace and suppressing any insurrection. Jesus, whose very presence garners crowds and who often questions the abuse by the authorities, presents a major threat to both parties.

Pontius Pilate's official residence was in the cosmopolitan seaport of Caesarea Maritima, Herod the Great's magnificent construction project. Within the amphitheater at the northern end was found a stone tablet incised with Pilate's name. From the Gospel accounts and Josephus, we know that Pilate went to Jerusalem only to strengthen the Roman presence among the crowds of pilgrims visiting the city during the Passover feast.

Pontius Pilate was not the weak, misinformed, and vacillating leader many think he was, and Luke notes his barbarity (13:1). The emphasis in this passage on Jesus' innocence is Luke's way of stressing that Jesus was not crucified for being a common insurrectionist (although that is the accusation), as many early Christian detractors at that time were saying.

In all of ancient literature, the only extant record of a Roman criminal court proceeding is the New Testament account of Jesus' trial before Pilate. Despite the variations of the trial among the four evangelists, their narrative lines are all quite similar: questioning by Pilate along with hesitancy on his part over Jesus' guilt; release of a criminal named Barabbas in Jesus' place; and a handing over of Jesus for crucifixion.

23:6-12 Jesus before Herod

Luke alone features this account. Herod Antipas, the son of Herod the Great, is the Jewish client-king of Galilee and Perea, and he is probably in Jerusalem for the Passover feast. Because Jesus is originally from Galilee, Pilate sends him to Herod as a diplomatic courtesy. The two leaders had been at enmity with each other, probably because of Pilate's slaughter of Galileans (13:1), but Pilate's action here reconciles the two.

Herod has an interest in Jesus (9:9), and it appears that he wishes to see some spectacle (23:8). Jesus never indulges in such displays. Consequently, Herod and his soldiers mock Jesus, as the Roman soldiers will do in 23:36. Jesus is returned to Pilate, where he is condemned. The Christian tradition sees this episode as a prophetic fulfillment of Psalm 2:1-2. See Acts 4:25-28.

23:13-25 The sentence of death

The Gospel presentation of a vacillating Pilate is most apparent in this scene. Any information about releasing a prisoner in honor of the holiday we have from Matthew, Mark, and John, but not Luke (ancient and dependable manuscripts omit v. 17, which appears to have been an added gloss prompted by the readings in Matthew 27:15 and Mark 15:6). Luke simply mentions that Pilate releases Barabbas (v. 25). The Gospels are the only source we have that mentions this custom; ancient Roman historians never refer to such a policy. Is Luke, or the other evangelists for that matter, relating a historical fact? Scholars are divided on the issue. In any case, the guilty Barabbas serves as a point of comparison with the innocent Jesus.

resplendent garb, he sent him back to Pilate. [12]Herod and Pilate became friends that very day, even though they had been enemies formerly. [13]Pilate then summoned the chief priests, the rulers, and the people [14]and said to them, "You brought this man to me and accused him of inciting the people to revolt. I have conducted my investigation in your presence and have not found this man guilty of the charges you have brought against him, [15]nor did Herod, for he sent him back to us. So no capital crime has been committed by him. [16]Therefore I shall have him flogged and then release him." [17]

The Sentence of Death

[18]But all together they shouted out, "Away with this man! Release Barabbas to us." [19](Now Barabbas had been imprisoned for a rebellion that had taken place in the city and for murder.) [20]Again Pilate addressed them, still wishing to release Jesus, [21]but they continued their shouting, "Crucify him! Crucify him!" [22]Pilate addressed them a third time, "What evil has this man done? I found him guilty of no capital crime. Therefore I shall have him flogged and then release him." [23]With loud shouts, however, they persisted in calling for his crucifixion, and their voices prevailed. [24]The verdict of Pilate was that their demand should be granted. [25]So he released the man who had been imprisoned for rebellion and murder, for whom they asked, and he handed Jesus over to them to deal with as they wished.

The Way of the Cross

[26]As they led him away they took hold of a certain Simon, a Cyrenian, who was coming in from the country; and after laying the cross on

continue

23:26-32 The way of the cross

Crucifixion was a feared form of execution that the Romans reserved for slaves, subject populations, and the lowest criminals. The vertical shaft of the cross usually remained him, they made him carry it behind Jesus. ²⁷A large crowd of people followed Jesus, including many women who mourned and lamented him. ²⁸Jesus turned to them and said, "Daughters of Jerusalem, do not weep for me; weep instead for yourselves and for your children, ²⁹for indeed, the days are coming when people will say, 'Blessed are the barren, the wombs that never bore and the breasts that never nursed.' ³⁰At that time people will say to the mountains, 'Fall upon us!' and to the hills, 'Cover us!' ³¹for if these things are done when the wood is green what will happen when it is dry?" ³²Now two others, both criminals, were led away with him to be executed.

The Crucifixion

³³When they came to the place called the Skull, they crucified him and the criminals there, one on his right, the other on his left. ³⁴[Then Jesus said, "Father, forgive them, they know not what they do."] They divided his garments by casting lots. ³⁵The people stood by and watched; the

continue

standing at the place of execution for successive use and to serve as a grim warning to the resident population. To add to their shame, the condemned were stripped naked and made to carry their own crossbeam amidst the jeers, taunts, and jabs of the crowd.

The Romans press Simon the Cyrenian into service, not because they pitied Jesus, but because they wanted to ensure that he lived long enough to undergo the ignominious death. By following behind Jesus, Simon becomes a model disciple, a point that would be important for the Cyrenians who formed part of the early Christian community (Acts 11:20; 13:1). The Gnostics, who denied the humanity of Jesus, will claim that Jesus was swept into heaven at the crucifixion and that Simon was mistakenly nailed to the cross, an interpretation that early Christian writers effectively counter.

People are following Jesus on the way (v. 27), and Luke's schism motif again surfaces; some are disciples, others are not. Luke often shows people divided along lines of discipleship, and this episode provides an example of that theme. The words to the "daughters of Jerusalem" (vv. 28-30), who bear a strong resemblance to a Greek chorus, reflect the scene described in the Lukan apocalyptic material (21:6-28). Here the context is one of forgiveness.

23:33-43 The crucifixion

Luke does not use the term "Golgatha"; he simply calls the area of crucifixion the "place called the Skull" (v. 33), which at the time of Christ was located outside the walls of Jerusalem. The spot of both the crucifixion and burial have been venerated as such since the second century, and the Basilica of the Holy Sepulchre has covered the place since the time of Empress Helena. The biblical, historical, and archaeological records confirm the area marked by the basilica as the true spot of Jesus' death, burial, and resurrection.

 Paradise is a Persian loanword ("park" or "garden") that here does not mean the Garden of Eden (Gen 2:8) but is a synonym for heaven.

In this section there is another bracketed verse: "Father, forgive them, they know not what they do" (23:34), probably one of the most gentle verses in the whole Bible. Nearly the same manuscripts that do not include 22:43-44 are the ones that also exclude this one. Although scholars are also divided on whether this verse should be part of the original text, a strong case can be made for its inclusion. In addition to its presence in dependable manuscripts, the verse certainly fits with the theme of forgiveness that runs through Luke's whole Gospel, including the passion (22:49-51).

While Luke has Herod's men alone ridiculing Jesus in 23:11, the evangelist situates the mocking by the Roman soldiers here at verses

36-37. Matthew and Mark mention that the two criminals revile Jesus, but only Luke provides a dialogue in which one criminal reprimands the other. At this point Jesus again utters words of mercy, and again we see the schism motif, with one criminal acknowledging Jesus and the other cursing him.

Throughout the crucifixion and death, there are intentional echoes from Psalm 22, Isaiah 53, Wisdom 2–3. These Old Testament works become the lens through which the kerygma is interpreted.

23:44-49 The death of Jesus

Luke's portrayal of the death of Jesus has important differences from the other two Synoptics. As the scene opens, we read of the description of the three hours of darkness. Luke adds the detail about the eclipse of the sun (v. 45). An eclipse is impossible during a full moon, which would have been the case during Passover. This verse should be read, therefore, as a circumstantial phrase well translated as "while the sun's light failed." If there is any historical background to three hours of darkness, it is most likely attributable to a dust storm coming from the desert, which is a common occurrence in this area during the spring of the year. The important point, however, is to see this passage as an echo of the many apocalyptic prophecies and writings that describe the Day of the Lord as one in which the sun will not shine (see Isa 13:10; Amos 8:9).

The tearing of the temple veil in Luke comes before the death of Jesus and not after it, as it does in Matthew and Mark. Luke is a fine literary artist, and by such a placement of the verse, he constructs the ripping of the curtain as a part of the buildup to the death of Jesus, the climax of the passage. The tearing of the veil itself is laden with a great deal of Old Testament symbolism. We really have no way of knowing to which of the several veils in the temple Luke (or the other evangelists) is referring. The bigger question is whether Luke sees the tearing as a means to let the divine presence out or the means to allow humans in. Since this Lukan version occurs before the death of Jesus,

rulers, meanwhile, sneered at him and said, "He saved others, let him save himself if he is the chosen one, the Messiah of God." [36]Even the soldiers jeered at him. As they approached to offer him wine [37]they called out, "If you are King of the Jews, save yourself." [38]Above him there was an inscription that read, "This is the King of the Jews." [39]Now one of the criminals hanging there reviled Jesus, saying, "Are you not the Messiah? Save yourself and us." [40]The other, however, rebuking him, said in reply, "Have you no fear of God, for you are subject to the same condemnation? [41]And indeed, we have been condemned justly, for the sentence we received corresponds to our crimes, but this man has done nothing criminal." [42]Then he said, "Jesus, remember me when you come into your kingdom." [43]He replied to him, "Amen, I say to you, today you will be with me in Paradise."

The Death of Jesus

[44]It was now about noon and darkness came over the whole land until three in the afternoon [45]because of an eclipse of the sun. Then the veil of

continue

letting the divine presence out is the better conclusion. This is the day of the Lord, and God's presence, his judgment, now centers on the cross.

Among the four Gospels, there are three versions of Jesus' last words from the cross. In each case Christ's final utterance is an expression of each evangelist's theology, which for Luke is trust in God. Jesus shows absolute confidence in the Father during this last moment, a mood quite different from his prayer on the Mount of Olives (22:39-46). With the word "Father," Luke connects this last prayer with the two other prayers Jesus has spoken throughout his passion: the agony (22:42) and the prayer for forgiveness (23:34). See also the prayer for the disciples (10:21) and the Lord's Prayer (11:2).

the temple was torn down the middle. ⁴⁶Jesus cried out in a loud voice, "Father, into your hands I commend my spirit"; and when he had said this he breathed his last. ⁴⁷The centurion who witnessed what had happened glorified God and said, "This man was innocent beyond doubt." ⁴⁸When all the people who had gathered for this spectacle saw what had happened, they returned home beating their breasts; ⁴⁹but all his acquaintances stood at a distance, including the women who had followed him from Galilee and saw these events.

The Burial of Jesus

⁵⁰Now there was a virtuous and righteous man named Joseph who, though he was a member of the council, ⁵¹had not consented to their plan of action. He came from the Jewish town of Arimathea and was awaiting the kingdom of God. ⁵²He went to Pilate and asked for the body of Jesus. ⁵³After he had taken the body down, he

continue

people; he separates the disciples and acquaintances from onlookers and mockers. The emphasis on the eyewitnesses will become an important point for the early church and will be used against those Gnostic detractors who would deny Jesus' actual death by crucifixion.

The Lukan proclivity to emphasize God's mercy becomes evident with the breast-beating onlookers as they return to their homes. The only other occurrence in Luke of breast-beating is in the parable of the Pharisee and the tax collector (18:9-14). In that parable the tax collector knows his sinfulness and asks for forgiveness. The onlookers, like the tax collector, know their sinfulness and depart asking for forgiveness. From Jesus' prayer from the cross, "Father, forgive them, they know not what they do" (23:34), we know that forgiveness is already there.

In Christian piety, verses 34, 43, and 46 are counted among the seven last words of Christ (see also Matt 27:46/Mark 15:34; John 19:26, 28, 30).

23:50-56 The burial of Jesus

The inclusion of the detail "a rock-hewn tomb in which no one had yet been buried," mentioned in some fashion in all four Gospels, underscores that Jesus' body is not laid in a tomb as part of a multiple burial. The evangelists stress that the tomb is new and unused. This detail later becomes important for the early church in countering Gnostic and Jewish charges that Jesus' body was confused among the corpses. All the activity has to be completed before the sabbath begins at sundown.

Joseph of Arimathea, like Simeon and Anna in the infancy narrative (2:25-38), awaits the "kingdom of God" (v. 51). With him, Jesus' universal message penetrates the Sanhedrin and, ironically, has a positive effect there. Joseph's concern for extending the legal prescriptions regarding burial of the dead ensures that Jesus is not totally excommunicated from his own nation. The women disciples from Galilee (8:1-3) are faithful throughout Jesus' ministry, are present at the crucifixion, and for the burial (v. 56).

The centurion offers the first reaction and therefore the first interpretation of Jesus' death in verse 47. The statement that Jesus is innocent (or righteous, just) recalls the deliberations of the Sanhedrin, Pilate, and Herod. On another level, the use of "innocent/righteous/just" harks back to the passage from Wisdom 3:1-3: "But the souls of the righteous are in the hand of God, / and no torment shall touch them. / They seemed, in the view of the foolish, to be dead; / and their passing away was thought an affliction / and their going forth from us, utter destruction. / But they are in peace." Luke sees the centurion's statement as an act of glorification of God. Jesus has accomplished his "exodus," which he set out to do in 9:31. The "hour . . . of darkness" (22:53) has passed; it is now the hour of the Lord's glorification, ushered in by Jesus' loud cry from the cross (v. 46), a paraphrase of Psalm 31:6.

In the last two verses of the death scene, Luke portrays another dichotomy among several

THE RESURRECTION

Luke 24:1-53

Discrepancies among the four Gospel accounts reflect the oral transmission of the stories. Each Gospel account relates the respective evangelist's theological interpretation of the fact that Jesus bodily rose on the first day of the week.

Resurrection accounts among the four Gospels can be arranged in several categories. First, there are those dealing with the empty tomb on the first day of the week. Second, there are Jesus' appearances in Jerusalem and environs. And third, there are his appearances in Galilee. All four Gospels feature accounts of the empty tomb, and, to a greater or lesser extent, they all recount appearances in Jerusalem. Luke's is the only one, however, that does not contain any narratives of the Galilean appearances. On the other hand, the most protracted Jerusalem story (24:13-35) is found only in the Third Gospel. Because the second volume to the Lukan corpus, the Acts of the Apostles, relates the whole missionary venture of the church as starting in Jerusalem and from there "throughout Judea and Samaria, to the ends of the earth" (Acts 1:8), Christ's presence in Galilee is simply folded into the broader picture with references to the spice-bearing women (23:55-56) and the "men of Galilee" (Acts 1:11).

24:1-12 The resurrection of Jesus

Tombs were often sealed with a large, wheel-like stone that was rolled in a carved trench in front of a rectangular doorway. Several strong men were needed to move it. The lowly status of women in ancient society not only kept them from politics, but it also meant that they were not to be taken seriously. Paradoxically, this condition gave them some power, since they could come and go in the most volatile areas without raising suspicion, as their standing at the crucifixion and their visit to the tomb attest. Mary Magdalene is the only woman witness common to all four Gospels. For this reason, she has been called

wrapped it in a linen cloth and laid him in a rock-hewn tomb in which no one had yet been buried. [54]It was the day of preparation, and the sabbath was about to begin. [55]The women who had come from Galilee with him followed behind, and when they had seen the tomb and the way in which his body was laid in it, [56]they returned and prepared spices and perfumed oils. Then they rested on the sabbath according to the commandment.

VIII: The Resurrection Narrative

CHAPTER 24

The Resurrection of Jesus

[1]But at daybreak on the first day of the week they took the spices they had prepared and went to the tomb. [2]They found the stone rolled away from the tomb; [3]but when they entered, they did not find the body of the Lord Jesus. [4]While they were puzzling over this, behold, two men in dazzling garments appeared to them. [5]They were terrified and bowed their faces to the ground. They said to them, "Why do you seek the living one among the dead? [6]He is not here, but he has been raised. Remember what he said to you while

continue

apostola apostolorum, the "apostle of the apostles."

That the stone has been rolled away when the women arrive is the first sign of something out of the ordinary. Luke has men, described in angel-like terms, stilling the women's fear and placing the resurrection in the context of Jesus' teaching and ministry. The men do not command the women to tell the others, but the women do so out of their own joy and enthusiasm, a truly Lukan ideal of the faithful disciple, and these women have not yet seen the risen Lord. Unfortunately, the men remain incredulous of the women's story, although Peter finds it sufficiently convincing to see for himself.

he was still in Galilee, [7]that the Son of Man must be handed over to sinners and be crucified, and rise on the third day." [8]And they remembered his words. [9]Then they returned from the tomb and announced all these things to the eleven and to all the others. [10]The women were Mary Magdalene, Joanna, and Mary the mother of James; the others who accompanied them also told this to the apostles, [11]but their story seemed like nonsense and they did not believe them. [12]But Peter got up and ran to the tomb, bent down, and saw the burial cloths alone; then he went home amazed at what had happened.

The Appearance on the Road to Emmaus

[13]Now that very day two of them were going to a village seven miles from Jerusalem called Emmaus, [14]and they were conversing about all the things that had occurred. [15]And it happened that while they were conversing and debating, Jesus himself drew near and walked with them, [16]but

continue

24:13-35 The road to Emmaus

The spice-bearing women have spread the word concerning the empty tomb, so the disciples in town know about it (24:9). One of the disciples along the road is called Cleopas (v. 18), a name similar to Klopas, the husband of one of the women at the cross, according to John's Gospel (19:25). Many have speculated with good reason that the two mentioned here are married to each other.

Luke is the only Gospel to present this passage, and there may be historical accuracy associated with it. At least three towns lay claim to being the Emmaus of this pericope. The text says that it is situated sixty stadia from Jerusalem, which is the distance for the round trip between the city and Emmaus, a walk one could make at that hour of the day, especially if as excited and enthusiastic as these two disciples. The Emmaus matching most of the criteria lies opposite present-day Moza, whose ruins from the 1948 war are still visible.

The reply to Jesus' questions summarizes the ministry as disciples would have seen and understood it (vv. 17-24). Jesus' explanation

Lessons while Traveling

In one of the most beloved passages of Scripture (Luke 24:13-35) we hear of disciples of Jesus who gradually shed their disappointment and fear to embrace the risen Lord. What happened to them as they traveled away from Jerusalem, no doubt intending to escape their dashed dreams and any possible dangers as followers of an executed criminal?

We know they talked. They *told stories* to each other, and to someone they believed to be a stranger traveling their direction. Their stories were a way of trying to make sense of what had happened, of trying to recover the meaning they felt in the presence of Jesus.

We know they attempted to *put the facts in order*. They retraced Jesus' ministry, his betrayal and gruesome death, and finally the report that Jesus' body was missing from the grave. Maybe they were searching for something they had missed or maybe they just wanted the stranger to know the facts before making a judgment.

We know they *listened to their fellow traveler*. They didn't argue with him when he expressed dismay and called them foolish, but in their listening they began to gain clarity.

We know they *offered hospitality*. Hospitality was a cardinal virtue in the ancient world and still is throughout the Middle East. Their generosity was a spontaneous and natural response to the relationship that had grown between them as they traveled.

We know they *saw with new eyes*, and in the breaking of the bread recognized Jesus in their midst.

Who knows what they learned as they traveled back to Jerusalem with lighter feet and the urgent message, "The Lord has truly been raised!"

places all the events within the context of Old Testament prophecies and Jewish experience (vv. 25-27). They recognize him in the breaking of the bread, a detail reiterated when they relate the story to the Eleven and the others. They can fully see who Jesus is, however, and therefore believe in him only once the "traveling companion" explains the Law and the prophets. None of this information is new to these disciples; they are merely hearing it again as though for the first time, and the little hope they may have had has blossomed into faith: "Were not our hearts burning [within us] while he spoke to us on the way and opened the scriptures to us?" (v. 32). This passage presents a balance between the word (vv. 25-27) and sacrament (vv. 30-32), and as such, it is highly eucharistic and liturgical. See also Mark 16:12-13.

By specifically using "eleven" (v. 33) instead of "apostles," Luke highlights Judas's betrayal and prepares the narrative for the election of his replacement in Acts 1:15-26.

24:36-49 The appearance in Jerusalem

Maintaining that the resurrected Jesus is a ghost is more comprehensible to the disciples than believing that he is risen. With this Jerusalem appearance, paralleled in John 19:19-29, Luke presents an apology for those who deny the reality of the resurrection. He does so by having Jesus call the question on the nature of his current existence (v. 39a). Jesus then allows the disciples to feel his flesh and bone while he presents the marks of the crucifixion (vv. 39b-40). Finally, he expresses hunger, and they give him fish to eat. Because it symbolizes overabundance, fish is a sign of the eschatological age, which Jesus' resurrection has indeed ushered in.

As he does with the disciples on the road to Emmaus, Jesus here explains his life, ministry, and resurrection in light of the Old Testament prophecies and experience. The role of the disciples as witnesses to these events is emphasized. They are to start in Jerusalem before heading to the nations. This geographical plan is restated in Acts 1:8. The "power from on high" (v. 49) is the Holy Spirit, who descends upon them in Jerusalem (Acts 2:1-13).

their eyes were prevented from recognizing him. [17]He asked them, "What are you discussing as you walk along?" They stopped, looking downcast. [18]One of them, named Cleopas, said to him in reply, "Are you the only visitor to Jerusalem who does not know of the things that have taken place there in these days?" [19]And he replied to them, "What sort of things?" They said to him, "The things that happened to Jesus the Nazarene, who was a prophet mighty in deed and word before God and all the people, [20]how our chief priests and rulers both handed him over to a sentence of death and crucified him. [21]But we were hoping that he would be the one to redeem Israel; and besides all this, it is now the third day since this took place. [22]Some women from our group, however, have astounded us: they were at the tomb early in the morning [23]and did not find his body; they came back and reported that they had indeed seen a vision of angels who announced that he was alive. [24]Then some of those with us went to the tomb and found things just as the women had described, but him they did not see." [25]And he said to them, "Oh, how foolish you are! How slow of heart to believe all that the prophets spoke! [26]Was it not necessary that the Messiah should suffer these things and enter into his glory?" [27]Then beginning with Moses and all the prophets, he interpreted to them what referred to him in all the scriptures. [28]As they approached the village to which they were going, he gave the impression that he was going on farther. [29]But they urged him, "Stay with us, for it is nearly evening and the day is almost over." So he went in to stay with them. [30]And it happened that, while he was with them at table, he took bread, said the blessing, broke it, and gave it to them. [31]With that their eyes were opened and they recognized him, but he vanished from their sight. [32]Then they said to each other, "Were not our hearts burning [within us] while he spoke to us on the way and opened the scriptures to us?" [33]So they set out at once and returned to Jerusalem where they found gathered together the eleven

continue

and those with them ³⁴who were saying, "The Lord has truly been raised and has appeared to Simon!" ³⁵Then the two recounted what had taken place on the way and how he was made known to them in the breaking of the bread.

The Appearance to the Disciples in Jerusalem

³⁶While they were still speaking about this, he stood in their midst and said to them, "Peace be with you." ³⁷But they were startled and terrified and thought that they were seeing a ghost. ³⁸Then he said to them, "Why are you troubled? And why do questions arise in your hearts? ³⁹Look at my hands and my feet, that it is I myself. Touch me and see, because a ghost does not have flesh and bones as you can see I have." ⁴⁰And as he said this, he showed them his hands and his feet. ⁴¹While they were still incredulous for joy and were amazed, he asked them, "Have you anything here to eat?" ⁴²They gave him a piece of baked fish; ⁴³he took it and ate it in front of them. ⁴⁴He said to them, "These are my words that I spoke to you while I was still with you, that everything written about me in the law of Moses and in the prophets and psalms must be fulfilled." ⁴⁵Then he opened their minds to understand the scriptures. ⁴⁶And he said to them, "Thus it is written that the Messiah would suffer and rise from the dead on the third day ⁴⁷and that repentance, for the forgiveness of sins, would be preached in his name to all the nations, beginning from Jerusalem. ⁴⁸You are witnesses of these things. ⁴⁹And [behold] I am sending the promise of my Father upon you; but stay in the city until you are clothed with power from on high."

The Ascension

⁵⁰Then he led them [out] as far as Bethany, raised his hands, and blessed them. ⁵¹As he blessed them he parted from them and was taken up to heaven. ⁵²They did him homage and then returned to Jerusalem with great joy, ⁵³and they were continually in the temple praising God.

This passage introduces the nature of the glorified body, a reality that goes to the heart of Christian belief. The resurrected life that Christ initiates goes beyond spiritual existence in eternity. It is a new life involving the glorified body that is not immediately recognizable to friends and loved ones, and therefore different from the mortal body, yet this glorified body has continuity with the mortal one. The glorified body transcends the limits of time and space, and yet it is physical. Wounds and blemishes are apparent, yet they do not scar or cause pain. Not much more can be said on the nature of the resurrected body than what Luke describes here. Luke wants faithful believers to know that the same destiny awaits them (see Acts 2:14-41).

24:50-53 The ascension

Luke recapitulates the ascension in the Acts of the Apostles (1:6-12), with some additions. The two ascension stories serve as a bridge connecting the two-volume work. Here it occurs on the same day as the resurrection; in Acts, it begins the apostolic ministry. This ascension account completes the journey to Jerusalem (9:51), while it also ends the Gospel. Jesus' exodus, first voiced in 9:31, is completed with the glorious ascension.

The road to Bethany passes over the Mount of Olives. Jesus was last on the mount during his agony and arrest, when the hour of the "power of darkness" held sway (22:53). His presence on the Mount of Olives now is the triumph over the dark power of Satan.

In Scripture, the Mount of Olives is considered the hill of God's judgment and glorification, and it takes on that role here. Jesus raises his hands in the Old Testament priestly blessing, he ascends gloriously into heaven, and the disciples are filled with joy. Although the Spirit does not come until they are gathered together at Pentecost (Acts 2:1-4), they participate even now in Christ's glorification by praising God in the temple (v. 53). They are the models for all Christians who await the fullness of Christ's reign.

EXPLORING LESSON FIVE

1. Why might both Roman and Jewish leaders consider Jesus a potential threat (23:1-25)?

_____

_____

_____

_____

2. Why has Herod had an interest in Jesus (23:8; see also 9:9)?

_____

_____

_____

_____

3. What do you think Jesus meant by telling the women of Jerusalem "to weep instead for yourselves . . . for if these things are done when the wood is green what will happen when it is dry" (23:28, 31)?

_____

_____

_____

_____

4. Only Luke provides the dialogue between the two criminals crucified beside Jesus (23:33, 39-40). How does their interaction reflect the schism motif found in Luke's gospel (see 2:29-32; 12:51-53)?

_____

_____

_____

_____

5. Why would it have been important to record that Jesus was buried in a tomb that had never been used before (23:53)?

_____

_____

_____

_____

_____

6. Why is "the apostle of the apostles" an appropriate title for Mary Magdalene (24:9-10)? (See John 20:11-18.)

_____

_____

_____

_____

_____

7. What aspects of the experience of the two disciples traveling to Emmaus are reflected in every Mass (24:13-32)?

_____

_____

_____

_____

8. How did Jesus' disciples obtain the ability to interpret the Old Testament as Christian Scripture (24:26-27, 44-45)? (See John 5:39; Acts 17:2-3; 1 Cor 15:3-4; 2 Tim 3:14-16.)

_____

_____

_____

_____

_____

9. What is "the promise of my father" that Jesus tells the disciples they must wait for in Jerusalem (24:49)? (See Acts 1:4-5; 2:1-4.)

_____

_____

_____

_____

10. What insights from the Gospel of Luke will you ponder and reflect upon further as a result of this study?

_____

_____

_____

_____

CLOSING PRAYER

Prayer

Then he opened their minds to understand the scriptures.   (Luke 24:45)

Jesus, victorious over death, teach us to seek life in all circumstances. Increase our understanding of the sacred words that proclaim the Good News so that we might be effective witnesses within a world sometimes plagued by death and division. We pray in thanksgiving for what we have learned, asking that our understanding lead to increased fervor to serve you . . .

PRAYING WITH YOUR GROUP

Because we know that the Bible allows us to hear God's voice, prayer provides the context for our study and sharing. By speaking and listening to God and each other, the discussion often grows to more deeply bond us to one another and to God.

At *the beginning and end of each lesson* simple prayers are provided for individual use, and also may be used within the group setting. Most of the closing prayers provided with each lesson relate directly to a theme from that lesson and encourage you to pray together for people and events in your local community.

Of course, there are many ways to center ourselves in God's presence as we gather together in groups around the word of God. We provide some additional suggestions here knowing you and your group will make prayer a priority as part of your gathering. These are simply alternative ways to pray if your group would like to try something different from those prayers provided in the previous pages.

Conversational Prayer

This form of prayer allows for the group members to pray in their own words in a way that is not intimidating. The group leader begins with Step One, inviting all to focus on the presence of Christ among them. After a few moments of quiet, the group leader invites anyone in the group to voice a prayer or two of thanksgiving; once that is complete, then anyone who has personal intentions may pray in their own words for their needs; finally, the group prays for the needs of others.

A suggested process:
In your own words, speak simple and short prayers to allow time for others to add their voices.

Focus on one "step" at a time, not worrying about praying for everything in your mental list at once.

Step One	Visualize Christ. Welcome him.
	Imagine him present with you in your group.
	Allow time for some silence.
Step Two	Gratitude opens our hearts.
	Use simple words such as, "Thank you, Lord, for . . ."
Step Three	Pray for your own needs knowing that others will pray with you.
	Be specific and honest.
	Use "I" and "me" language.

Step Four	Pray for others by name, with love.
	You may voice your agreement ("Yes, Lord").
	End with gratitude for sharing concerns.

Praying Like Ignatius

St. Ignatius Loyola, whose life and ministry is the foundation of the Jesuit community, invites us to enter into Scripture texts in order to experience the scenes, especially scenes of the gospels or other narrative parts of Scripture. Simply put, this is a method of creatively imagining the scene, viewing it from the inside, and asking God to meet you there. Most often, this is a personal form of prayer, but in a group setting, some of its elements can be helpful if you allow time for this process.

A suggested process:

- Select a scene from the chapters in the particular lesson.
- Read that scene out loud in the group, followed by some quiet time.
- Ask group members to place themselves in the scene (as a character, or as an onlooker) so that they can imagine the emotions, responses, and thinking that may have taken place. Notice the details and the tone, and imagine the interaction with the Lord that is taking place.
- Share with the group any insights that came to you in this quiet imagining.
- Allow each person in the group to thank God for some insight and to pray about some request that may have surfaced.

Sacred Reading (or Lectio Divina)

This method of prayer invites us to "listen with the ear of the heart" as St. Benedict's rule would say. We listen to the words and the phrasing, asking God to speak to our innermost being. Again, this method of prayer is most often used in an individual setting but may also be used in an adapted way within a group.

A suggested process:

- Select a scene from the chapters in the particular lesson.
- Read the scene out loud in the group, perhaps two times.
- Ask group members to ponder a word or phrase that stands out to them.
- The group members could then simply speak the word or phrase as a kind of litany of what was meaningful for your group.
- Allow time for more silence to ponder the words that were heard, asking God to reveal to you what message you are meant to hear, how God is speaking to you.
- Follow up with spoken intentions at the close of this group time.

REFLECTING ON SCRIPTURE

Reading Scripture is an opportunity not simply to learn new information but to listen to God who loves you. Pray that the same Holy Spirit who guided the formation of Scripture will inspire you to correctly understand what you read, and empower you to make what you read a part of your life.

The inspired word of God contains layers of meaning. As you make your way through passages of Scripture, whether studying a book of the Bible or focusing on a biblical theme, you may find it helpful to ask yourself these four questions:

What does the Scripture passage say?
Read the passage slowly and reflectively. Become familiar with it. If the passage you are reading is a narrative, carefully observe the characters and the plot. Use your imagination to picture the scene or enter into it.

What does the Scripture passage mean?
Read the footnotes in your Bible and the commentary provided to help you understand what the sacred writers intended and what God wants to communicate by means of their words.

What does the Scripture passage mean to me?
Meditate on the passage. God's word is living and powerful. What is God saying to you? How does the Scripture passage apply to your life today?

What am I going to do about it?
Try to discover how God may be challenging you in this passage. An encounter with God contains a challenge to know God's will and follow it more closely in daily life. Ask the Holy Spirit to inspire not only your mind but your life with this living word.